302.12.

Social Cognition looks at the way in which humans interpret, analyse and remember information about their social world. Topics covered include: attribution, social schemas and social representations, prejudice and discrimination.

Donald C. Pennington is a Chief Examiner for A-level Psychology and Pro-Vice Chancellor at Coventry University.

Routledge Modular Psychology

Series editors: Cara Flanagan is a Reviser for AS and A2 psychology and lectures at Inverness College. Philip Banyard is Associate Senior Lecturer in Psychology at Nottingham Trent University and the Chief Examiner for OCR psychology. Both are experienced writers.

The *Routledge Modular Psychology* series is a completely new approach to introductory level psychology, tailor-made to the new modular style of teaching. Each short book covers a topic in more detail than any large textbook can, allowing teacher and student to select material exactly to suit any particular course or project.

The books have been written especially for those students new to higher-level study, whether at school, college or university. They include specially designed features to help with technique, such as a model essay at an average level with an examiner's comments to show how extra marks can be gained. The authors are all examiners and teachers at the introductory level.

The *Routledge Modular Psychology* texts are all user-friendly and accessible and include the following features:

- practice essays with specialist commentary to show how to achieve a higher grade
- chapter summaries to assist with revision
- progress and review exercises
- glossary of key terms
- summaries of key research
- further reading to stimulate ongoing study and research
- cross-referencing to other books in the series

Also available in this series (titles listed by syllabus section):

ATYPICAL DEVELOPMENT AND ABNORMAL BEHAVIOUR

Psychopathology
John D. Stirling and Jonathan S.E. Hellewell

Therapeutic Approaches in Psychology
Susan Cave

BIO-PSYCHOLOGY

Cortical Functions
John Stirling

The Physiological Basis of Behaviour: Neural and hormonal processes
Kevin Silber

Awareness: Biorhythms, sleep and dreaming
Evie Bentley

COGNITIVE PSYCHOLOGY

Memory and Forgetting
John Henderson

Perception: Theory, development and organisation
Paul Rookes and Jane Willson

DEVELOPMENTAL PSYCHOLOGY

Early Socialisation: Sociability and attachment
Cara Flanagan

PERSPECTIVES AND RESEARCH

Controversies in Psychology
Philip Banyard

Ethical Issues in Psychology
Mike Cardwell (forthcoming)

Introducing Research and Data in Psychology: A guide to methods and analysis
Ann Searle

Theoretical Approaches in Psychology
Matt Jarvis

SOCIAL PSYCHOLOGY

Social Influences
Kevin Wren

Interpersonal Relationships
Diana Dwyer

OTHER TITLES

Sport Psychology
Matt Jarvis

Health Psychology
Anthony Curtis

Psychology and Work
Christine Hodson (forthcoming)

STUDY GUIDE

Exam Success in AEB Psychology
Paul Humphreys

Social
Cognition

Donald C. Pennington

London and Philadelphia

First published 2000
by Routledge
11 New Fetter Lane, London EC4P 4EE

Simultaneously published in the USA and Canada
by Taylor & Francis Inc.
325 Chestnut Street, Suite 800, Philadelphia, PA 19106

Routledge is an imprint of the Taylor & Francis Group

© 2000 Donald C. Pennington

Typeset in Times and Frutiger by Keystroke,
Jacaranda Lodge, Wolverhampton
Printed and bound in Great Britain by
TJ International Ltd, Padstow, Cornwall

British Library Cataloguing in Publication Data
A catalogue record for this book is available from the British Library

Library of Congress Cataloging in Publication Data
Pennington, Donald C.
Social cognition / Donald C. Pennington.
p.   cm. — (Routledge modular psychology)
Includes bibliographical references and index.
1. Social perception. I. Title. II. Series.
HM1041 .P46 2000
302'.12–dc21   00–032172

ISBN 0–415–21704–0 (hbk)
ISBN 0–415–21705–9 (pbk)

To Isabel, of course
and
Blob, who else?

Contents

Illustrations

Acknowledgements

I have enjoyed writing this book. The more so since I completed some of the chapters on a work/holiday in Porthleven, Cornwall. So thanks to the house overlooking the harbour and the pubs in the evening. I spent this time with my daughter, Kyla, who was revising for her university examinations at the time. She helped and commented at times, and dragged me down the pub at other times. So thanks to Kyla.

Cara Flanagan and Vivien Ward have been most helpful on advice and guidance to ensure this book is consistent with the housestyle for this Modular Psychology series. So thanks to Cara and Vivien.

Finally, my thanks to Kathleen Williams who has typed, formatted, and offered invaluable, helpful advice to make the whole book, especially the figures and tables, look really good. So thanks to Kathleen.

The series editors and Routledge acknowledge the expert help of Paul Humphreys, Examiner and Reviser for A-level Psychology, in compiling the Study Aids chapter of each book in the series.

They also acknowledge the Assessment and Qualifications Alliance (AQA) for granting permission to use their examination material. The AQA do not accept responsibility for the answers or examiner comment in the Study Aids chapter of this book or any other book in the series.

Introduction to social cognition

What is social cognition?

One of the defining features that sets human beings apart from other animals is not only our ability to think, but also our ability to be aware of what we are thinking. A second feature, although shared with some other animal species, is our sociability and the central importance we place on relationships with other people. Put these two features together and you have the heart of what **social cognition** is about. Definitions are often useful and one that is particularly helpful characterises social cognition as:

> The manner in which we interpret, analyse and remember information about the social world.
>
> (Baron and Byrne, 1997)

This definition highlights three cognitive processes that we apply to our social world. First, information we receive about other people (and ourselves, for that matter) is *interpreted*; this means that information is given meaning often by both the social context and our previous experience, cultural values, etc. Rarely do we interpret another person's behaviour in a vacuum; what we know about the person – associated stereotypes, social groups to which he or she may belong – all feed into the interpretation made. Second, social information is *analysed*, this means that an initial interpretation may be adjusted, changed or even rejected. For example, whilst the first impression we make of another person may be unduly influential, further acquaintance and interaction with the person may dramatically change this impression. Third, social information is *stored in memory* from which it may be recalled or retrieved. Recalling information from memory may require considerable effort; effort that we may not always be willing to make. The final comment to make about this definition of social cognition is that the 'social world' refers *both* to other people and ourselves. Theory and research in social cognition may equally be about other people, ourselves, and, which is most likely, about ourselves in interaction with other people.

Progress exercise

Think about someone you often hear about and read about in the national newspapers or on television. This may be Tony Blair (the Prime Minister), or Bill Gates (head of Microsoft), or another well-known figure. Write down what you can recall from memory about this person then consider this information in relation to interpretations and analyses that have been made.

Social psychologists who research into social cognition commonly investigate such questions as:

- What caused a person to behave in a particular way?
- Why does somebody laugh in one social situation and behave in an unfriendly way in another situation?
- How do we mentally represent what we know about another person or group of people?

- How does belonging to a social group affect how we behave to others who are members of the same group, and others who are not group members?
- Why do individuals and groups of people engage in discrimination and conflict with other groups of people?
- How can prejudice and conflict between people be reduced?

Social cognition and social psychology

Our definition of social cognition means that most areas covered by social psychologists may be included. However, areas which are more concerned with social factors, those external to the person, rather than internal factors (or those related to characteristics of the person) are:

- The relationship between a person's attitudes and how he or she actually behaves.
- The development, maintenance and breakdown of relationships between people.
- Small group behaviour, including decision-making, leadership, group norms and roles.
- Social influence processes including majority and minority influence, and obedience to authority.

These areas of social psychology tend to focus on social factors which are *external* to the person, unlike **social cognition** which is concerned with internal factors and related mental processes. General text books on social psychology (for example, the further reading suggestions at the end of this chapter) do cover a much wider range of topic areas in social psychology. Other texts in the Modular Psychology series on Social Influences (Kevin Wren), Interpersonal Relationships (Diana Dwyer), and Pro- and Anti-Social Behaviour (David Clarke, forthcoming) cover some key topics in social psychology. However, it could be argued that all areas should and can be considered from the perspective of social cognition.

Social cognition and cognitive psychology

In a sense, social cognition may be considered to be a sub-area of cognitive psychology. However, cognitive psychologists do not limit themselves to mental processes solely to do with people. At the heart of cognitive psychology are interests in memory, forgetting, perception and information processing more generally (see other books in this series by Henderson, 1999; and Rookes and Willson, 1999). However, as Fiske and Taylor (1991) point out, people are not simply another object of study by cognitive psychologists. The main reasons are that people are causal agents in ways inanimate objects, or even other animals, are not; people have awareness and self-awareness; people are extremely complex not only physically but especially psychologically; and people grow psychologically and change over time.

Social cognition borrows many ideas and themes from cognitive psychology, but is unique because of the interest in combining these themes to the study of people in social settings.

Identify one difference and one similarity between social cognition and cognitive psychology.

Historical perspective

Psychology, particularly in the United States of America, was dominated by the behaviourist approach between the 1920s and the 1950s. Pavlov's classical and Skinner's operant conditioning, with rewards and punishments, had no time for mental processes and actively discouraged their investigation. However, two psychologists in America and one in Britain laid the foundations for the social cognition approach which is so dominant in social psychology today. These three pioneers were Solomon Asch, Fritz Heider and Frederick Bartlett.

Asch, perhaps one of the most famous social psychologists, was an advocate of the **Gestalt** approach in psychology. The Gestalt psychologists believed that 'the whole is greater than the sum of the parts'. This put them into direct opposition to the behaviourists who claimed that all behaviour could be explained from the building blocks of stimulus–response linkages (i.e. the individual, component parts). Asch translated the Gestalt approach to social psychology by investigating how we form impressions of other people. Basically, Asch (1946) claimed that certain personality traits are 'central' to the impression we form, whilst others are 'peripheral'. One central personality dimension is that of warm–cold. Being told that a person is 'cold' has much more influence on the impression we form than being told a person is, for example, practical.

Fritz Heider published a highly influential book in 1958 entitled *The Psychology of Interpersonal Relations*. Heider, also an advocate of Gestalt psychology, likened human mental processes to that of a 'naïve scientist'. That is, people attempt to predict, understand and control their social worlds by trying to understand what causes people to behave in the ways that they do. This parallels with what scientists do in physics, chemistry and biology. Heider distinguished between causes within the person (traits or personality dispositions) and causes in the situation (for example, social pressure or peer pressure to conform). This laid the foundations for the hugely important area of **attribution theory** in social cognition.

Frederick Bartlett was primarily interested in memory, and again influenced by the ideas of Gestalt psychology. His best-known and influential research concerned how we remember stories; he used stories such as 'War of the Ghosts' in which people were asked to read a short passage then write down what they could remember about it. Bartlett (1932) introduced the term **schema** to characterise a knowledge structure, in this case of the story, that is represented mentally. Social schemas, as we shall see in Chapter 4, are of great importance for understanding how we represent our social world. Social schemas are also important for understanding stereotyping.

These three psychologists – Asch, Heider and Bartlett – made the study of mental processes respectable in a time when behaviourism was dominant. Their work laid the foundations for modern social cognition.

Three principles of social cognition

The chapters that follow consider theory and research on attribution and attributional errors, social perception, and prejudice and discrimination. Three themes or principles will recur from time to time as you work through these chapters: people as cognitive misers; spontaneous versus deliberative thought; and the importance of self-esteem. We will briefly look at each here.

People as cognitive misers

Fundamental to cognitive psychology and social cognition is the idea that people are limited in their ability and capacity to process information. Because of this, either shortcuts to information processing may be taken or people may be unwilling to expend a lot of mental effort to think about something. Shortcuts that people commonly use represent simple rules of thumb or strategies to deal with potentially complex information. These shortcuts are efficient in terms of time and mental effort, but because they are shortcuts they may often lead to errors and biases. The **cognitive miser** may be characterised as trading-off accuracy and thoroughness for speed, a quick decision or judgement and use of minimal mental effort.

Everybody acts as a cognitive miser at some time or another; in practical terms you could not function if you did try to attend to and process all the information you receive about your social world. The pitfalls and dangers of the cognitive miser are, to some extent, offset by the experience and knowledge we have of our social world. Hence, social schemas may be employed to help us make a quick decision or judgement in the face of complex and large amounts of information.

Spontaneous and deliberative thought

We have just seen that cognitive misers use strategies to simplify judgements and decision-making, and one of these may be to employ social schemas. When a similar social situation occurs again and again, or when there are perceived similarities between different social situations, a person's response may be spontaneous since it is so well-learned that it is automatic. Gilbert (1989) distinguished between **spontaneous** and **deliberative** social thought. When people use spontaneous or automatic thought, mental effort and time is kept to a minimum, and efficiency is obtained. However, 'top of the head' thinking may be superficial and erroneous on occasions and not always to be encouraged.

Deliberative thought is where a person takes time, makes a conscious mental effort and thinks things through more deeply before coming to a judgement or decision. Social psychologists have identified two main factors which determine whether spontaneous or deliberative thought will be used. These are motivation and ability (Fazio, 1990). If you lack motivation or are preoccupied by other tasks then spontaneous thought is most likely. If you are motivated to find out more or think about matters more fully, deliberative thought will result. Likewise with ability, if you are able and knowledgeable about a particular matter you are more likely to engage in deliberative thought. Although you may notice the tendency for experts to provide quick answers on occasions as well, this is probably because they know what they are talking about so well that they often do not need to think or deliberate before speaking.

Self-esteem

It may seem strange to mention **self-esteem** as a guiding principle of social cognition. However, the evaluation we make of ourselves is central to social cognition since how we think about ourselves is highly influenced by how other people talk and behave towards us. A person with high self-esteem perceives him or herself to be capable, have self-worth and is usually confident with other people. A person with low self-esteem may be the opposite, with the result that he or she may lack motivation. One consequence of this is that deliberative thought may be avoided. Also, as we shall see in Chapter 5, our social identification with social groups and the esteem in which groups are held also have consequences for our own self-esteem or self-evaluation. We will want to identify with and belong to a social group that is well-regarded and held in high esteem by others. We will also want to avoid identifying with a group held in low esteem, although this may not always be possible. **Social identity theory** (see Chapter 5) attempts to explain and understand prejudice and conflict between groups on the basis of how one group treats another. This is based on individual self-esteem and self-evaluation.

Critical comment

Social cognition is a particular approach in social psychology that puts heavy emphasis on how we represent social knowledge and mentally process social information. You may think that the approach is too inward-looking and ignores social forces and social pressures that do not require such a 'mentalistic' approach. For example, to explain why people conform to a majority, or obey an authority figure, do you really need to bring in social cognitions? Situational factors and forces can often have an overwhelming influence on behaviour, and hence substantially reduce the importance of social cognitions.

Much of the research that is described or referred to in this book draws on laboratory-based experimental procedures. It is often claimed that due to low **ecological validity** (the experimental situation does not reflect our everyday social world) and the artificiality of such research settings, experimental findings cannot be readily generalised to everyday social life. You need to make your own mind up about this, and engage in considerable deliberative thought rather than voice someone else's point of view!

> **Review exercise**
>
> Think about the amount of work you do in your study of psychology. Identify areas where you act as a cognitive miser: which areas of psychology interest you and hence engage you in deliberative thought, and how well you regard yourself as a student of psychology compared to other psychology students in your class.

About this book

Chapters 2 to 5 present theory and research in the core areas of social cognition. Chapter 2 considers the basic concepts and theories of the attribution approach by detailing the correspondent inference theory, the covariation model, causal schemata model, and Weiner's model of attribution for success and failure. Chapter 3 looks at accuracy and error in how we attribute causality to behaviour and pays particular attention to the fundamental attribution error, actor–observer differences, and self-serving biases. Both these chapters consider cross-cultural differences in attribution. Chapter 4 deals with the broad area of social perception looking at impression formation, considers different types of social schemas (person, self, role and event schemas), strategies of the cognitive miser, and social representations. Chapter 5 covers prejudice, discrimination, and intergroup conflict from both social cognitive and individual perspectives. Consideration of attempts to reduce prejudice and conflict by social psychologists is also provided. Chapter 6 looks at up-to-date issues in social cognition including how children develop attributions of their own and other people's behaviour and their development of social representations. Two extensions of prejudice are considered: terror management theory and everyday communications. Finally, two applications of attribution theory are considered in relation to health and sport. It is not really intended that you read this chapter as a whole, but that you dip into a section once you have read one or more of Chapters 2–5. Signposts will be given to you in these chapters when it may be best to dip into one of these sections in Chapter 6.

Each chapter presents theory and research with diagrams and tables to show main findings and figures to summarise what has been said. The latter are intended to provide you with revision aids. Chapter 7 provides study aids to help you prepare for examinations.

Each chapter ends with a summary and suggestions for further reading. A glossary of key words and terms is provided at the end of the book.

Summary

Social cognition may be defined as the ways in which we interpret, analyse, and remember information about ourselves and other people. Social cognition is a sub-area of social psychology and draws heavily on ideas and concepts in cognitive psychology. Three themes in social cognition are: the person as a cognitive miser; spontaneous versus deliberative thought; and the importance of self-esteem.

Further reading

Dwyer, D. (2000) *Interpersonal Relationships*, London: Routledge. Another book in this modular psychology series that provides a sustained consideration of how we make, maintain and deal with the breakdown of social relationships.

Fiske, S. and Taylor, S. (1991) *Social Cognition*, 2nd edn, New York: McGraw-Hill.

Regarded as the authoritative text on social cognition. A little dated now, but does present the main themes, theories and influential research in social cognition in a readable manner. An advanced, but accessible text.

Pennington, D. C., Gillen, K. and Hill, P. (1999) *Social Psychology*, London: Arnold.
Introductory text which provides representative coverage of the major areas of social psychology theory and research. Deals extensively with social cognition.

Wren, K. (1999) *Social Influences*, London: Routledge.
Another book in this modular psychology series that provides a detailed look at social influence and highlights the importance of external pressures (peers, authority figures, etc.) to conform and obey.

2

Attribution of causality I: concepts and theories

What are attributions?

Imagine that you have just read about a case in the newspaper where a woman had been convicted of the manslaughter of her husband and yet had been given just a suspended sentence. The woman had suffered years of abuse from her husband and was not able to put up with it any longer; this resulted in her stabbing him to death. Why did she kill her husband?

Your best friend, you have recently discovered, has lied to you about her whereabouts last Saturday night. For months both of you had planned to go to a concert and had reserved tickets at the theatre. On the Friday night your best friend rang to say that she could not go out with you because she had to stay in to babysit for her parents. In fact she went out to the nightclub with other friends. Why did your friend behave like this towards you?

You have just taken a mock psychology examination and been told by your teacher that you have not done very well. This surprises you since you had been revising for weeks for the examination. How do you explain your poor performance?

Each of these three examples requires an explanation of someone's behaviour. In doing this you may infer or make a judgement about the cause of the behaviour. **Causal attributions** help us to understand our own and other people's behaviour. People have a very strong tendency to provide a causal explanation for virtually any act or behaviour – quite often this is achieved with little conscious thought. Heider (1958) initiated the development of the attribution approach in social psychology. He proposed that the main reason people make causal explanations is to help them predict and control their social worlds. If we can successfully explain past behaviour, the chances are that the same or similar causes will allow us to predict what people may actually do in future social situations.

In this chapter we will consider four important attribution theories: the correspondent inference theory of Jones and Davis (1965), Kelley's (1967) covariation model, the causal schemata model (Kelley, 1972) and Weiner's (1979) model of attributions for success and failure. Following this we will look at differences in how attributions are made between individuals and cultures. In Chapter 3 we will consider how people actually attribute causes to events and how errors and biases are often revealed.

The basics

Baron and Byrne (1997) define causal attribution as:

> The process through which we seek to identify the causes of others' behaviour and so gain knowledge of their stable traits and dispositions.
>
> (p. 50)

This is a useful definition, but omits to make reference to both the social situation in which the behaviour takes place, and that people are as concerned to explain their own behaviour (either to themselves or other people) as they are to explain other people's behaviour.

Nevertheless, this definition does highlight the fact that causal explanations are made in relation to personality characteristics, traits and dispositions of the individual.

Internal and external causes

Consider our first example of the woman killing her husband. Was this caused by some negative aspect of her personality or was it a response to an unendurable situation? In the language of attribution a **dispositional (internal)** attribution means that the behaviour is best explained by reference to the person's temperament, personality, emotional state, i.e. something internal to the person. By contrast, a **situational (external)** attribution means that the behaviour is best understood as a response to pressures exerted by the situation, i.e. something external to the person. A dispositional (internal) explanation for the woman killing her husband could be that she was cold-hearted, hated her husband and had planned to kill him for some time. A situational (external) explanation might focus on the persistent abuse that her husband had shown over the years and that anyone might do the same in this situation. Since the woman was convicted of manslaughter and given a very light sentence, you might reasonably infer that the jury and judge gave greater weight to a situational rather than dispositional set of causes. Notice with this example that the type of attribution made has consequences for how responsible a person is seen to be for their actions. Here the apparent situational pressures were so great that we reduce our perception of the woman's responsibility for her actions. Figure 2.1 summarises possible internal and external attributions to explain the second example of your best friend's dishonest behaviour.

Think of a recent social situation in which you had a disagreement with a friend. Identify two situational (external) and two dispositional (internal) causes of your behaviour.

Progress exercise

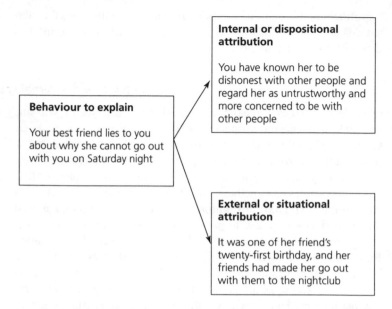

Behaviour to explain

Your best friend lies to you about why she cannot go out with you on Saturday night

Internal or dispositional attribution

You have known her to be dishonest with other people and regard her as untrustworthy and more concerned to be with other people

External or situational attribution

It was one of her friend's twenty-first birthday, and her friends had made her go out with them to the nightclub

Figure 2.1 Internal and external attributions to explain the cause of your best friend lying to you

Spontaneous and deliberative attributions

All behaviour, our own and other people's, may be a candidate for causal attribution. However, you do not spend all your time thinking about or trying to work out a causal explanation. Sometimes we make an attribution **spontaneously**, i.e. without thinking about it. Stereotypes and impressions we hold may result in a spontaneous attribution. For example, some people may hold the stereotype that old age is associated with physical and mental deterioration: this may lead to a person spontaneously attributing the cause of 'senility' to a 75 year-old forgetting their personal identification number for their bank account. This explanation might be sufficient for the person, and be made without further thought or consideration about specific events in the older person's life. For example, imagine that your friend has told you that someone, who has just joined your psychology class and is unknown to you, has a very extrovert personality. This may lead you to use this disposition or trait to explain the behaviour of this person, without considering the stranger on his or her own merits. From these two examples, you can see that spontaneous attributions may not properly take account of an individual's actual behaviour.

When you think about the person's behaviour and the social context in which it takes place before making a causal attribution you are being **deliberative**. Making a deliberative attribution takes time and mental effort, but ensures that you think carefully before you decide on the cause(s) of a person's behaviour. Two factors have been shown to encourage deliberation: these are motivation and ability (Fiske and Neuberg, 1990). If you are not motivated or too busy to spend time thinking, then a spontaneous attribution will be made. Oddly enough, it has been found that people in a good or happy mood are more likely to make spontaneous attributions (Hamilton and Mackie, 1993). This occurs, presumably, because engaging in mental effort to think more deeply about someone's behaviour may take you out of being in a happy mood. A spontaneous attribution maintains the good mood. Figure 2.2 summarises, using an example, what has been said above about spontaneous and deliberative attributions.

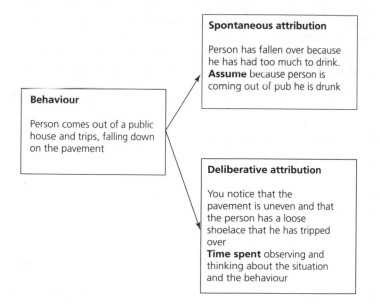

Figure 2.2 **Spontaneous and deliberative causal attributions for the same behaviour**

Imagine you have been introduced to a Hell's Angel motorcyclist by your friend. Identify three dispositional or personality traits that spontaneously come to mind about Hell's Angels. Then consider why these should or should not apply to any one individual.

Voluntary and non-voluntary behaviour

Social behaviour may sometimes be intended and planned, whilst at other times accidental and not under our voluntary control. Kruglanski (1975) made a distinction between actions (planned, voluntary behaviour) and occurrences (unplanned, involuntary behaviour). Kruglanski then went on to claim that actions should be given internal causal attributions, whilst occurrences may be given either internal or external explanations. Affective or emotionally based behaviour is usually seen as not under voluntary control, i.e. it is an occurrence, and hence may attract both internal and external attributions.

This distinction between voluntary (planned) and non-voluntary (unplanned) behaviour is useful; it applies to our first example of the woman killing her husband. This basic judgement about the behaviour has consequences for how we perceive the woman's responsibility for the act.

Theories of attribution

Correspondent inference theory

The correspondent inference theory of Jones and Davis (1965) is solely concerned with the conditions under which we make dispositional (internal) attributions of another person's behaviour. That is, how we infer corresponding dispositions of an individual which offer a causal explanation of their behaviour. That is, how we observe behaviour and *infer* a corresponding disposition, thus providing a causal explanation for the behaviour. Dispositions (traits) of a person are stable and enduring aspects of personality: hence, knowing a person's dispositions will allow you to predict how he or she should behave in future.

Jones and Davis (1965) state that information is required about five factors in order to make correspondent inferences. First, the person's behaviour must be voluntary and chosen freely; we cannot infer much about behaviour that somebody had little choice over since it is likely that most people would behave in the same way. Second, does the behaviour produce **non-common effects**? This means is there something about the consequences of the behaviour that is unexpected or a specific outcome of only that behaviour. For example, suppose there are two cinemas, both roughly the same distance from where you live and both showing the same film that you want to see. Cinema A sells a brand of ice cream that you like, whilst Cinema B does not. You choose to go to Cinema A. The non-common effect of this behaviour is that you get the ice cream that you like! Third, for a dispositional inference to be made the behaviour should not be seen as socially desirable. When a person does something that is against norms or conventions you can usually be sure that it reflects something about the person. Socially desirable behaviour does not single out one person from another, since the desire to please other people often overrides how we are as individuals (Baumeister and Leary, 1995). Fourth, if somebody else's behaviour has an impact on the person making the attribution it is said to have **hedonic relevance**. Hedonic relevant behaviour is intended to affect, positively or negatively, the person making the attribution: it is said to have personalism. Again, personally relevant behaviour will lead to dispositional or correspondent inferences being made. Figure 2.3 details the example of a person choosing a university to go to and the type of inference that may be made.

Think of a recent example of where you have had to make a difficult choice, for example, which university to apply to, which nightclub to go to. Try to identify each of the five factors required for a correspondent inference. Are there factors you cannot identify? If so, why may this be the case?

Progress exercise

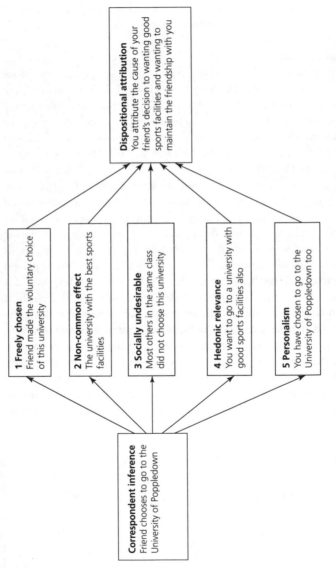

Correspondent inference
Friend chooses to go to the University of Poppledown

1 Freely chosen
Friend made the voluntary choice of this university

2 Non-common effect
The university with the best sports facilities

3 Socially undesirable
Most others in the same class did not choose this university

4 Hedonic relevance
You want to go to a university with good sports facilities also

5 Personalism
You have chosen to go to the University of Poppledown too

Dispositional attribution
You attribute the cause of your friend's decision to wanting good sports facilities and wanting to maintain the friendship with you

Figure 2.3 **The correspondent inference model of Jones and Davis (1965) showing how five types of information are used to make a dispositional attribution**

Evaluation

The theory of Jones and Davis (1965) does suffer from a number of limitations. For example, the theory assumes that the attributor is able correctly to categorise the behaviour as voluntary – this may require informed knowledge of the person. Also, if we have information about the five factors identified above it is unlikely to be available all at one time – consider the difficulties you had with the last progress exercise. As information becomes available we correct or update the dispositional attribution made (Gilbert *et al.*, 1988). A more general shortcoming is the assumption Jones and Davis make that people are able to process all these five types of information and combine them to form a causal explanation. As we saw in Chapter 1, people are limited in their ability to process information. This may result in errors or biases, which we shall explore more fully in Chapter 3. Finally, the major limitation is that the correspondent inference theory only deals with making dispositional (internal) attributions. Thus, the theory ignores situational (external) attributions, and behaviours which may require both types of attributions.

The covariation model

The covariation model of Kelley (1967) has wider use than the correspondent inference model since it accounts for both dispositional (internal) and situational (external) attributions, as well as special circumstance attributions. It is called the covariation model since Kelley claims that three types of information are used, and how these covary determines the type of attribution made. The three types of information are **consistency**, **distinctiveness**, and **consensus**, and each can have a high or low value.

The best way to understand the model is through an example of behaviour: Jennifer takes a major part in discussion in a particular psychology class. Consistency information is concerned with whether Jennifer takes part in discussion in the other psychology classes that she attends. If she does, then consistency is high (Jennifer takes part in discussion in most psychology classes); if she does not, then consistency is low (Jennifer rarely takes part in discussion in other psychology classes). Distinctiveness information asks whether Jennifer takes part in discussion in classes on different subjects (English, mathematics, etc.). If she does, then distinctiveness is low – this means there is nothing unusual about Jennifer discussing a lot in psychology classes. If she does not, then distinctiveness is high – this means that there is something unusual about Jennifer discussing a lot in psychology classes. Finally, consensus information asks what other people do – in this example, do other people take part in discussion in psychology classes also? If they do, consensus is high, if they do not consensus is low. These three types of information, each with a high or low value produce sixteen separate combinations. Figure 2.4 shows when an internal or external attribution is made.

A **circumstance** attribution is made when distinctiveness is high, consistency low and consensus low. For example, Jennifer only took part in discussion in this class, whereas others did not take part in discussion, because it was her birthday and she was very excited.

Progress exercise

Imagine you have been to the cinema with some friends to see a comedy film. You did not find it very funny and did not laugh much. Your friends and most of the audience did laugh a lot. Identify, in relation to your own behaviour, consistency, distinctiveness, and consensus information. Then try to speculate about why you did not find the film very funny.

Evaluation

Numerous empirical studies have lent support to the covariation model (McArthur, 1972; Cheu *et al.*, 1988), however consensus information seems to be the least used by people when making attributions (Kruglanski, 1977). Making a causal attribution on the basis of consistency, distinctiveness and consensus information demands considerable effort or deliberative thinking on the part of the individual. Sometimes not all three types of information are available and at other times we may be simply too busy to give sufficient attention to inferring a cause. Baron and Byrne (1997) claim that situations where an unexpected event or behaviour occurs, and unwanted, negative outcomes result, are most likely to lead a person to use these three types of information. That is, everyday, common events do not evoke the use of these types of information.

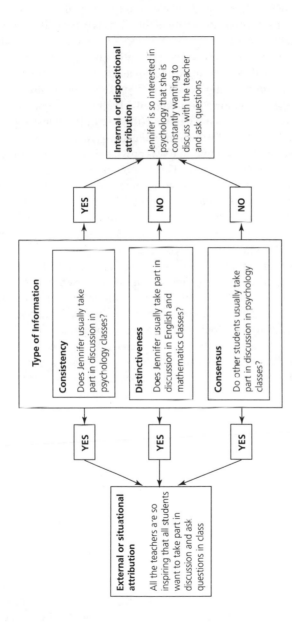

Figure 2.4 The use of consistency, distinctiveness and consensus information in making an internal or external attribution. (Start with the middle column – Type of Information)

However, there will be occasions when consistency, distinctiveness and consensus information are not available. This is especially the case when we observe one-off or single instances of behaviour and so do not have information about how the person has behaved in the past. Kelley (1972) stated that for single instances people rely on either a **discounting** or **augmenting** principle to make a causal inference. To highlight the discounting principle take the first example, at the beginning of this chapter, of the woman convicted of the manslaughter of her husband. Without further knowledge you may speculate on a number of causes, for example, she was provoked, it was an accident, she suffered a mental disorder. The discounting principle is 'the tendency to attach less importance to one potential cause of behaviour when other potential causes are also present' (Baron and Byrne, 1997). In our example, you may discount the mental illness and the accident explanations in favour of her being provoked. Such an explanation may fit in with other similar cases that you know about.

The augmenting principle is 'the tendency to attach greater importance to a cause if the behaviour occurs in the presence of inhibiting factors (Baron and Byrne, 1997). For example, suppose you are told that Toby has achieved 80 per cent in an advanced mathematics examination. You will no doubt think he is good at mathematics. You then find out that Toby is only 15! This latter information augments your initial dispositional attribution (Toby is good at mathematics) to lead you to say that he is a genius at mathematics. The contributory factor in this case is age since we do not expect someone of 15 years to be so good at advanced mathematics.

Finally, Kelley's covariation model may have a limited range of application since the three types of information are not always available to the attributor. Furthermore, there is research which reports that people find it difficult to assess covariation (Alloy and Tabachnik, 1984). Also, we have seen how the discounting and augmenting principles may be used by a person observing a one-off event. Kelley (1972) developed the idea of **causal schemas** to explain how we make attributions in the absence of detailed information or for a single event.

Causal schemata model

A causal schema is 'a general conception the person has about how certain kinds of causes interact to produce a specific kind of effect'

(Kelley, 1972). This means that our past experiences of causes and their effects allow us to develop abstract generalisations that can then be applied to a specific event. One such abstraction is the 'multiple necessary causes schema', which is when we know from previous experience that at least two causes must be present. For example, being interviewed for and offered a job as a fashion model implies previous training and good acting skills, as well as an appropriate physical appearance.

Hannah has recently been offered a job at a vegetarian restaurant. To get the job she had to demonstrate good knowledge of vegetarian food and good interpersonal skills with customers. Identify the multiple necessary causes schema that are present here.

Progress exercise

Evaluation

Causal schemas are generally regarded as important because they allow attributions to be made in the absence of detailed information. They also represent underlying ideas that we have about cause–effect relationships and may reflect stereotypical views. A further advantage is that causal schemas allow an individual to make an attribution quickly and with little cognitive effort. However, these strengths are also weaknesses since a 'snap' judgement about the cause of some-one's behaviour may be incorrect or biased. In more extreme cases a causal schema may reflect prejudicial opinions. In the end causal schemas may reflect little more than prevailing stereotypes and attitudes that are held by society or a sub-culture at a specific time.

Based on the limitations identified with each of these three attribution theories, list the limitations or weaknesses of each and identify which you think has the best application to a wide range of behaviour. State your reasons for this.

Review exercise

Weiner's model of attributions for success and failure

Imagine that you have just handed in a psychology essay and you are waiting for it to be marked. The mark you receive will allow you to make a judgement about your relative success or failure in psychology. This is an all too familiar situation for students and one that relates closely to Weiner's (1979, 1986) model of causal attribution for success or failure. If you receive a good mark you will be happy, but if you receive a poor mark you may be upset. Either way, Weiner claims, you will make a causal attribution for your performance and from this generate expectations for future performance. This is the basis of Weiner's model and is depicted in Figure 2.5.

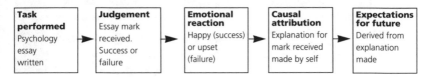

Figure 2.5 Weiner's model for achievement

In making a causal attribution for success or failure (achievement) Weiner claims that we use three dimensions to produce a range of different causes to explain achievement. These three dimensions are locus, stability and controllability. **Locus** refers to whether the achievement is more to do with the person (internal) or situation (external). **Stability** is to do with whether the internal or external factor is stable, that is enduring and likely to be present in the future, or unstable. If it is unstable then it may only apply to one situation and hence not be present at other times. **Controllability** concerns the extent to which the person believes or perceives his or her performance to be under personal control.

Each dimension has two categories which yield eight different types of cause to explain achievement. For example, suppose you have received a very high mark for your psychology essay: you are very happy over this since you worked very hard on the essay, as you usually do. This causal attribution can be translated into Weiner's dimensions as internal, stable and controllable. That is, it was to do with you (internal), that you put a lot of effort in (controllable) and this reflects how you normally work (stable). Figure 2.6 shows the different

	Internal		External	
	Stable	**Unstable**	**Stable**	**Unstable**
Controllable	Typical effort	Special effort	Help or hindrance from others	Special help or hindrance from others
Uncontrollable	Ability	Mood	Task difficulty	Chance or luck

Figure 2.6 **Weiner's (1986) three dimensions of locus, stability and controllability, with the eight associated attributions**

attributions associated with the eight possible combinations. Note from a 'typical effort' attribution you would predict that other essays you write for psychology in the future will also attract good marks.

The model depicted in Figure 2.6 does make certain assumptions, for example, ability is characterised as internal, stable and uncontrollable. If you think of ability in terms of intelligence the model seems to imply that there is not much you can do about your level of intelligence – implying a biological or genetic explanation. Many educational psychologists would disagree and argue that motivation, education and help from other people can change a person's intelligence level. The model also assumes that the mood we are in is something that is unstable (which is correct since our mood changes very rapidly sometimes) and uncontrollable. It is questionable how much control we can have over our moods, for example, health psychologists demonstrate that regular exercise makes us feel happier (Taylor, 1995).

Attributing success or failure for an examination performance to luck (external, unstable, and uncontrollable) reflects the feeling that luck is something we can do little about. In the context of an examination a 'luck attribution' for good performance might be along the lines 'I was lucky because the right questions came up.' Or for failure, 'I was unlucky because the areas I revised did not come up as questions.' It may be though, that someone who has done well in an examination is making a 'luck' attribution due to modesty. What someone says to another person about the causes of their success may differ from what the person privately believes or thinks. This may be a problem for Weiner's model since it does not take into account overarching factors such as social norms or social desirability.

Evaluation

Weiner's model has implications for how teachers treat their students. The dimension of controllability may be especially important, for example, when a teacher believes some students to be very able but they do not achieve high marks. Here the teacher may attribute the students' poor performance to lack of effort and because of this try to get the students to work harder. Effort is seen as within the control of these students by the teacher.

Weiner (1995) has developed this model to encompass attributions of responsibility and blame. From looking at Figure 2.6 it is relatively easy to see that if we attribute the cause of behaviour underlying an incident (for example, a motor car accident) to internal, controllable and either stable or unstable causes, then we are going to hold the driver responsible for the incident and its consequences.

Weiner's model of attribution for success and failure has received widespread empirical support in many different contexts, but particularly in education and the law. Social psychologists have, however, questioned how important the dimension of controllability is in relation to that of locus and stability (Fiske and Taylor, 1991). One of the enduring strengths of the model is that it shows how attribution and emotional response may be linked.

Comparison of the theories

The four different attribution theories we have just considered are not to be seen as offering competing explanations of how we attribute causes to behaviour. They are best seen as being applicable in different circumstances. For example, the correspondent inference theory applies only when you are interested in the conditions under which dispositional (internal) attributions are made. By contrast, Kelley's covariation model is only of use when you have a considerable amount of information about how the person has acted over a period of time, how other people act in similar situations and how the person acts in different situations. The covariation model requires deliberative thought as does the correspondent inference theory. By contrast, the causal schemata model relies upon schema built up from past experience and hence may operate more spontaneously in our thought. Finally, Weiner's model for achievement is concerned with how we attribute the causes of success and failure to our own or other people's achievements.

These theories have been accepted within social psychology for over thirty years and are supported by a considerable amount of empirical research – conducted both in the laboratory and in field settings. They also enjoy a wide range of valuable applications – as shown in Chapter 6 where applications to health and sport are considered.

Consider the last essay you wrote for psychology and the mark you received for it. Analyse this in relation to locus, stability, and controllability. Following this decide whether the mark you received was fair or unfair.

Progress exercise

Individual differences

Up to this point we have considered different theories of attribution which ignore how one individual may differ from another. Is there a personality factor or set of factors showing that different people display tendencies to attribute causes to different events in a similar way? Theory and research on this issue can be traced back over 30 years to Rotter's (1966) work on **locus of control**.

Rotter (1966, 1982) distinguished between internal and external locus of control. His work developed from a behaviourist tradition, whereby people with an internal locus of control believe they have personal control over rewards and punishments that they receive. By contrast, people with an external locus of control believe that things happen to them and they have little or no control over the rewards and punishments they experience. Translating this into the language of attribution, people with an external locus of control will attribute causes of events in their lives to luck, fate or the actions of powerful others. This means that externals perceive little relationship between their own behaviour and efforts and what happens to them. This has parallels with Weiner's (1986) dimension of controllability since, for example, in both Weiner's and Rotter's models attributing failure in an examination to bad luck (the wrong questions came up) is external and not in the control of the person.

People who show an internal locus of control personality will see, for example, success in an examination as due to the effort they put in when revising prior to the examination. Research on locus of control has shown that those who score as internal tend to achieve better in education (Mooney *et al.*, 1991). However, people who score very high as internals over-attribute failure to themselves (Phares, 1976) and perceive other people as being more responsible for their actions than is warranted. One consequence of this may be that internals are less sympathetic and severe in their judgements about others who do wrong.

Rotter developed a questionnaire to assess where, on a continuum of 0 to 25, any one individual scored. The locus of control questionnaire employed a forced-choice approach, which means that you are given two options and have to agree with one of them (this is in contrast to a multiple choice or free-choice type of questionnaire). Figure 2.7

		Locus of control items
1	(a)	Many of the unhappy things in people's lives are partly due to bad luck
	(b)	People's misfortunes result from mistakes they make
2	(a)	In my case getting what I want has little or nothing to do with luck
	(b)	Many times we might just as well decide what to do by flipping a coin
3	(a)	In the case of the well-prepared student, there is rarely, if ever, such a thing as an unfair test
	(b)	Many times exam questions tend to be so unrelated to coursework that studying is really useless

Figure 2.7 **Examples from Rotter's (1966) locus of control questionnaire. To score, add up the statements with (a) or (b) underlined (only underlined letters score points). High score indicates external locus of control, a low score, internal**

presents three items from this scale. You may be interested to score yourself on these questions to get an indication of which type you might be.

Research has shown that as people get older they tend to become more internally orientated (Lefcourt, 1982). A word of warning, however, in that you can be too far up the internal or external end of the scale. For example, Smith *et al.* (1983) showed that those scoring as very high internals may become what we call 'control freaks'. Here such people have unrealistic beliefs about how much they can control their behaviour. At the other extreme, very high scores on the external side may reflect low self-esteem and high levels of anxiety in a person (Holder and Levi, 1988).

Evaluation

As we have seen, there are parallels between Rotter's idea of locus of control and Weiner's dimension of controllability. A questionnaire widely used to investigate how those suffering depression attribute the causes of events is the attributional style questionnaire (Seligman *et al.*, 1979). A depressive attributional style is characterised by making external and uncontrollable explanations for events. This leads to feelings of helplessness with an associated perception that however hard you try you cannot change things.

One great strength of this approach is that it does focus on how individuals may differ in the attributions they make and why this may be so. The theories of attribution that we have previously considered all ignore differences in personality between people.

Cultural differences

Social psychologists investigating differences between cultures have consistently found that people in Western cultures tend to have a more individual or independent approach to life, whilst people in Eastern cultures emphasise interdependence among each other, or collectivism (Smith and Harris Bond, 1998). Typically white Americans or white British people emphasise personal identity whilst Chinese emphasise social identity (Triandis, McCusker and Hui, 1990). This might lead you to infer that people who are part of an individualistic culture will emphasise dispositional (internal) attributions when explaining behaviour. In contrast people from collectivist cultures will emphasise situational (external) attributions. Social psychologists have investigated this empirically and findings have broadly upheld these predicted attributional differences.

Morris and Peng (1994) asked American students and Chinese students who were studying in the United States to read summaries of two murders that had recently been reported in the newspapers. One murder concerned a Chinese student who had not succeeded in getting an academic job at a top US university. The other concerned a white American postman who shot his boss. In both cases the murderers ended up shooting themselves. American and Chinese students were asked to indicate, on rating scales, likely dispositional and situational causes for the murderers' behaviour. For example, dispositional causes included mental illness, need to control everything, and personality defect. Situational causes included economic recession, violence on the television, and American values such as selfishness.

Results showed that Americans rated dispositional attributions as more important than situational explanations. By contrast, and as predicted, Chinese students rated situational explanations as more important. These resulted are depicted in Figure 2.8. Interestingly this difference was present for both types of students regardless of whether the murderer was American or Chinese. Morris and Peng (1994) also

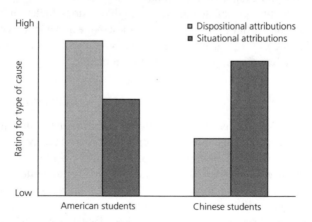

Figure 2.8 **Dispositional and situational attributions for murder made by American and Chinese students**
Source: **Adapted from Morris and Peng, 1994**

analysed accounts of the murders as reported in English and Chinese newspapers. The same dispositional/situational differences in explanation were found in these reports.

Cross-cultural differences in attributions have also been investigated by analysing free descriptions that people give to behaviour. The free descriptions are then analysed for the number of dispositional and situational explanations given. This approach has some advantage over using rating scales, as in the study described above, since a person's own account of another's behaviour should reflect more accurately their social cognitions. Rating scales impose content and structure on a person and so may not reflect how a person actually thinks and attributes causes.

To investigate this, Miller (1984) gave American and Indian participants a number of single paragraph descriptions of different incidents. For example, the following account of a motorcycle accident was one such paragraph:

> The rear wheel burst on the motorcycle. The passenger sitting on the rear jumped. The moment the passenger fell he struck his head on the pavement. The driver of the motorcycle, who is an attorney, took the passenger to a local hospital and went on and attended his court work. The driver left the passenger there without consulting the doctor about the seriousness of the injury – the gravity of the situation – whether the passenger should be shifted immediately – and he went on to court. Ultimately the passenger died.

Miller (1984) analysed the free-response explanations given by Americans and Indians to this scenario and listed the three most common given by each group. These are shown in Figure 2.9.

As you can see Americans most frequently cited trait or dispositional attributions and Indians situational or context attributions. Other research by Miller (1984) showed that Americans use three times as many dispositional attributions as Indians. On the other hand, Indians use twice as many situational or context explanations as Americans.

Most frequent American attributions	Most frequent Indian attributions
• Driver was irresponsible	• Driver's duty to be in court for his client
• Driver was in a state of shock	• Incident made the driver confused
• Driver was aggressive in pursuit of his career	• Injured passsenger did not look seriously hurt

Figure 2.9 **Dispositional and situational explanations given for the motorcyclist's behaviour in Miller's (1984) study**

In summary, good evidence has been found to support the claim that cross-cultural differences in attributions exist. People from individualist or independent cultures (such as the United States, Great Britain) emphasise trait or dispositional attributions. By contrast, people from collectivist or interdependent cultures emphasise situational or context attributions.

Overall evaluation of concepts and models

The attribution approach is modelled on the idea that people operate like naïve scientists (Heider, 1958). This implies that people are seen to be systematic, rational and logical in the way causes are attributed to behaviour. Much evidence has been accumulated across social psychology which seriously questions this assumption. For example, in attitude research it has been shown that people often defend the attitude they hold when evidence tells them that they are wrong to do so. Likewise in attribution research people are often biased or make errors in causal explanation. The next chapter is largely devoted to errors and biases, so not much more need be said here.

The attribution models/theories that have been considered in this chapter are all **normative** theories; this means that they prescribe what should normally be the type of attribution made (dispositional or situational) given that certain types of information are present. However, Hilton and Slugoski (1986) criticise these models since they fail to take account of the knowledge a person already possesses and do not consider the types of relationship that may exist between the person making the attribution and the person whom the attribution is about. To deal with these criticisms Hilton and Slugoski (1986) have proposed an **abnormal condition model**. The basic idea here is that people possess knowledge and experience which leads them to expect certain behaviours in specific social situations. People, they claim, only really make efforts at causal explanations when something abnormal happens. In such circumstances the question to be answered is 'Why did this happen rather than the norm?' Take the example, given at the start of this chapter, about your best friend lying to you. You would regard this as an abnormal condition since you would expect your best friend to be open and honest with you (that is what best friends should be and why they are best friends!). In such cases, claim Hilton and Slugoski (1986), an explanation of what caused your best friend to act in this way is of vital importance to you and an explanation must be found. The incident threatens your relationship and needs to be cleared up so that you can decide whether to stay best friends.

Another criticism of these models of attribution is that they are assumed to apply universally and across cultures. Early research by Garland *et al.* (1975) demonstrated that when given the opportunity to ask for information other than consistency, distinctiveness or consensus, people ask about personality characteristics, situations in which the behaviour took place and other information about the person such as age, marital status, type of employment.

On the positive side, these models of attribution do enjoy a wide range of application – from atypical behaviour to psychology and the law. Chapter 6 looks at how psychologists have applied attribution theory and concepts to health and sport. You may wish to dip into one or both of these now.

Jasmin comes from a culture that may be characterised as 'collectivist'. She also exhibits a high level of locus of control. Jasmin has recently won a debating competition in which she had to defend the importance of psychology in the modern world. How might the concepts of collectivist culture and locus of control affect the attributions that could be made for her behaviour? Consider this in relation to someone from a non-collectivist culture and who has a low level of locus of control.

Review exercise

In summary, these models of attribution often do not take account of what people actually do. As we shall see in the next chapter, error and bias, in relation to these normative models, is often present in the actual causal explanations we make for our own and other people's behaviour.

Summary

Attribution is the process through which we attempt to explain the causes of our own and other people's behaviour as dispositional or situational causes. Dispositional causes relate to traits about the person; situational causes to the forces outside of the person and to do with the context in which the behaviour takes place. Attributions are sometimes made spontaneously with little thought being required, and sometimes deliberatively where effort and thought are needed. The correspondent inference model of Jones and Davis is concerned with conditions under which dispositional attributions are made. Kelley's covariation model considers how distinctiveness, consistency and consensus information is used to make internal, external and circumstance attributions. The causal schemata model applies when only very limited information is available and applies to only a single event.

Weiner's model proposes that the dimensions of locus, stability, and controllability determine the type of attribution made for success or failure. People show individual differences in attributing causes and this has been related to Rotter's ideas of internal and external locus of control. Cross-cultural differences in attributing causes have used the concepts of individual and collectivistic cultures to show how the former emphasise dispositional and the latter situational explanations.

Criticisms of the models of attribution are to do with questioning whether they apply universally, and whether they actually reflect the way people make attributions.

Further reading

Fiske, S. T. and Taylor, S. E. (1991) *Social Cognition*, 2nd edn, New York: McGraw-Hill.
The 'bible' for theory, research, critical comment and thoroughness of coverage. Very detailed in places, but quite readable. Needs a third edition quite urgently as it is nearly a decade old now. A source book that covers all aspects fully.

Lord, C. G. (1997) *Social Psychology*, Fort Worth: Harcourt Brace College Publishers.

Written by one of the leading American researchers in social cognition, and attribution theory in particular. Develops the ideas of spontaneous and deliberative thinking in relation to making causal attributions. Uses numerous applied examples related to health, law and education.

Smith, P. B. and Harris Bond, M. (1998) *Social Psychology Across Cultures*, 2nd edn, London: Prentice Hall.

Second edition of classic text dealing with all aspects of cross-cultural theory and research in social psychology. Provides a chapter on social cognition with numerous cross-cultural empirical studies reported, some in detail.

3

Attribution of causality II: accuracy and error

Causal inferences and accuracy

Imagine that you have just had a major row with your intimate partner (boyfriend, girlfriend, husband, wife, etc.), where you have each accused the other of being at fault. You say, 'You're always working so hard then going out in the evening so that I never get to see you.' Your partner says, 'You never want to do anything and I like to be busy and out with other people.' You then provide an attribution to your partner along the lines of being gregarious, never able to keep still, always wanting to be busy. These are dispositional (internal) attributions. Your partner provides causal explanations of his or her behaviour along the lines of being asked to go out socially and feeling obliged, being given too much work to do which simply has to be done and never being asked out by you. These are situational (external) attributions. As you can see from this imaginary disagreement there are basic differences in attributions made by you about your partner, and by your partner about his or her behaviour. Who is right? Or put a different way, whose attributions are accurate and whose inaccurate?

This is not an easy question to answer and for the two people involved the differences may be difficult to resolve. One way of attempting to assess accuracy and error would be to have some kind of objective standard by which to compare the two sets of attributions. However, unlike the world of physics and chemistry, this does not exist in social psychology. Another way might be to have a set of norms or frame of reference which captures what most people normally do. But what is the norm does not mean it is right, or that commonly made attributions are accurate. Another way might be to construct theories and models of causal attribution and then see if attributions that people make are consistent or deviate from such models. In general, this latter approach has been the one adopted by social psychologists investigating errors and biases in attribution processes.

In this chapter we shall consider four well-researched and important errors that people demonstrate when attributing causes to either their own or other people's behaviour. These are: the fundamental attribution error; actor–observer biases; the false consensus effect and self-serving biases. We will then consider how people attribute responsibility. Finally, the chapter looks at cross-cultural differences with respect to attributional biases and errors.

The fundamental attribution error

At the start of Chapter 2 we considered the imaginary case of a woman who killed her husband and was then convicted of manslaughter. You might imagine the press giving banner headlines such as 'Evil wife slaughters husband' or 'Callous and uncaring wife kills husband in a fit of rage'. These headlines are making dispositional attributions about the personality of the woman. The headlines have ignored situational factors such as the abuse that the woman had put up with for years. Concentrating on dispositions/personality characteristics of a person to the virtual exclusion of situational factors is what social psychologists have called the **fundamental attribution error**.

Put another way, the fundamental attribution error is the tendency to overestimate the importance of dispositions and to underestimate the importance of situational factors when attributing causes to another person's behaviour (Ross and Nisbett, 1991). The error is regarded as a fundamental one since it is assumed to be pervasive and occur across a wide range of behaviours. Gilbert and Malone (1995) characterise it as a marked tendency for people to regard situational factors and influences as invisible or non-existent. It is important to realise that the error only applies when making causal attributions about somebody else's behaviour. It does not apply when making attributions about your own behaviour. This will be taken up more fully when we come to consider actor–observer differences on pages 43–6.

A classic study demonstrating this error was conducted by Ross *et al.* (1977). College students were recruited for an experiment in which some played the role of questioner and others the role of contestant in a general knowledge quiz game. Who became questioner and contestant was randomly decided by students drawing cards. Instead of the questioner asking pre-determined questions, participants were each given 15 minutes in which to make up their own general knowledge questions. This clearly advantaged the questioner and disadvantaged the contestant since the general knowledge would reflect what the questioner knew and would be idiosyncratic to him or her. After the quiz questioners and contestants were asked to rate each other's general knowledge. Ross *et al.* also had another group of college students observe the quiz; these observers were asked to rate the level of general knowledge of both questioners and contestants.

As can be seen from Figure 3.1, questioners thought that they knew more general knowledge than contestants (but the difference was not significant). By contrast, contestants rated their own general knowledge as low and that of the questioner as high. Observers, who knew that questioners made up their questions, ignored the situational constraints and rated the general knowledge of the questioner as very high and that of contestant as low. This experiment offers a compelling demonstration of the fundamental attribution error since strong dispositional attributions about levels of general knowledge were made of questioner and contestant which reflected little consideration of the strong advantage given to the questioner in this situation.

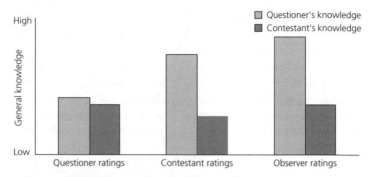

Figure 3.1 **Ratings of general knowledge of questioner and contestant after quiz game by questioners, contestants and observers**
Source: **Adapted from Ross** *et al.* **(1977)**

Evaluation

Numerous explanations have been put forward by social psychologists for the fundamental attribution error; we shall consider two of the more important ones here. First is the recognition, originally by Heider (1958), that another person's behaviour 'engulfs our perceptual field'. That is, as an observer of another's behaviour we focus our attention on the person him- or herself rather than pay attention to the social situation in which the behaviour takes place. Factors such as the social context, a person's role, and situational pressures are less likely to occupy our thought and attention than what the person is actually doing. As Fiske and Taylor (1991) express it 'because the person is dominant in the perceiver's thinking, aspects of the person come to be overrated as causally important' (p. 67).

Progress exercise

Consider a courtroom television programme and think about the defendant who is on trial. The prosecution case is often dominated by negative and criminal characteristics of the defendant, with the aim of trying to show he or she is a dishonest person. Videotape the programme and list examples of what you consider to be the fundamental attribution error.

This explanation has led some social psychologists to regard the error as a result of spontaneous rather than deliberative thought (see Chapter 2). Gilbert (1989) has suggested a two-stage model in which automatic or spontaneous dispositional attributions are first made and then adjusted through a deliberative stage.

Imagine again the case of the wife killing her husband and people's explanation of this. According to Gilbert this might be as follows:

- Stage 1: Spontaneous dispositional attribution – the woman was uncaring, unable to control her temper and aggressive.
- Stage 2: Deliberative attribution – her husband had abused her physically and emotionally for years causing her to be at the end of her tether and go mad.

However, Gilbert claims that situational factors are often difficult to incorporate in the process and are more complex to understand. This results in the original, spontaneous attribution being confirmed. Gilbert *et al.* (1988) demonstrated support for this two-stage model in an experiment in which participants in one condition were distracted or 'cognitively busy', and those in another condition not distracted. All participants watched a video of a woman who demonstrated anxious behaviour (biting nails, tapping fingers, running hands through her hair). Half of the participants were told the woman had been discussing topics that made her anxious, and the other half were told that neutral topics, such as travel, had been discussed. Participants in the 'distracted' condition were asked to memorise material, whilst those in the 'undistracted' condition were not asked to memorise material. Results clearly showed that distracted participants attributed high levels of anxiety to the woman regardless of the topic of conversation. By contrast, those who had not been distracted took account of the different topics of discussion and rated the woman as less dispositionally anxious in the 'anxious' condition of the experiment. The results showed clear support for the two-stage model explaining the fundamental attribution error; the model is shown in Figure 3.2.

Using Figure 3.2 think of a behaviour of a friend (for example, phoning you to ask you out, working together on a psychology assignment, finishing with his or her boyfriend/girlfriend). Think about causes for this behaviour by filling in the boxes in Figure 3.2. Hint: a distraction might be your watching television or going out with another friend.

Progress exercise

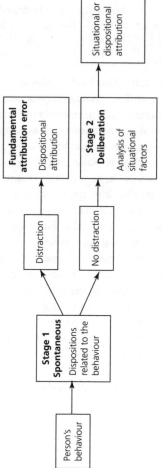

Figure 3.2 **Two-stage model of the fundamental attribution error**
Source: **After Gilbert, 1989**

It is interesting to note that the logic of this model means that strategies which encourage people to consider, or make more salient, situational factors should reduce the tendency for people to make the fundamental attribution error.

Actor–observer differences

Consider again the example given at the start of this chapter about you having a row with your partner. You make dispositional attributions and your partner makes situational attributions. From the perspective of your partner this demonstrates the classic actor–observer differences when making causal explanations. Social psychologists have produced a wealth of evidence demonstrating that when explaining your own behaviour (actor) there tends to be an emphasis on situational factors, and when explaining another person's behaviour (observer) the emphasis is on dispositional factors (Jones and Nisbett, 1972). A series of experiments conducted by Nisbett et al. (1973), which investigated attributions concerning, for example, choice of subject of academic study, offered support for actor–observer differences. Here participants were asked to explain why they had chosen to study psychology at university as well as why they thought their friends had chosen to study psychology. Attributions to self reflected dispositions (for example, interested in people, keen to have a career using psychology). By contrast, attributions to others reflected situational factors (for example, quality of the course, status of the university, good sports facilities).

Extensions to the original claims have been made by, for example, Baxter and Goldberg (1988) who suggest that actors see their own behaviour as less stable and predictable in comparison to how somebody else's behaviour is perceived. This may reflect that we are more aware of our own mood changes, emotions and behavioural inconsistencies because these experiences are not directly accessible to us in other people. How another person is feeling may be effectively masked by what that person does or says.

Why should this actor–observer difference exist? One explanation is that when explaining our own behaviour our attention is more focused on situation constraints and how other people influence us. By contrast, when explaining another's behaviour our attention is focused on the behaviour. This latter explanation is similar to that for the fundamental attribution error. If this is the case then making situational factors more salient for the observer and dispositional factors more salient for the actor should reverse the actor–observer difference.

Reversing actor–observer differences

A classic study by Storms (1973) showed how actor–observer differences could be reversed by changing the orientation of the attributor. In this experiment pairs of participants engaged in conversation whilst two other participants observed – one watching one participant and one watching the other participant. Half of the participants who had engaged in conversation were shown a videotape of themselves, and the observer who had been instructed to watch this person was shown the same video tape. This was the *same orientation* condition in the experiment. In the *opposite orientation* condition the other half of the participants were shown a video of the other person in conversation.

The results are depicted in Figure 3.3, and show quite clearly that participants in the same orientation condition displayed the traditional actor–observer differences. In contrast, participants in the opposite orientation condition whilst tending towards dispositional explanations, displayed many more situational explanations.

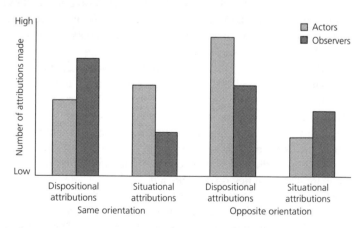

Figure 3.3 **Dispositional and situational attributions for actors and observers in the same and opposite orientations**
Source: Adapted from Storms, 1973

Imagine you have just received a poor mark for your psychology essay. Make up a traditional 'actor' explanation in terms of situational factors. Now go to your bedroom and look at yourself in the mirror, think of the same imaginary essay. Do you find it easier to make dispositional attributions about yourself when looking at yourself in the mirror? This is similar to one of the actor 'opposite orientations' in the experiment by Storms (1973).

Progress exercise

Other factors that have been found to reverse the traditional actor–observer difference are positive behaviours (such as being helpful to another person), when an actor knows he or she (the actor) has a certain disposition (for example, being a friendly person), and through empathy instructions (where you are asked to imagine yourself to be the other person) (Fiske and Taylor, 1991). For example, asking a person to observe another by pretending it is themselves actually behaving, results in more dispositional attributions being made (Cheu *et al.*, 1988).

Evaluation

Whilst evidence exists for actor–observer differences in causal explanation, actors do not exhibit an absolute preference for situational explanations. The results of the experiments by Storms (1973), depicted in Figure 3.3, show this since actors in the same orientation condition (viewing themselves on video tape) make many dispositional attributions as well. Furthermore, attributions about another's behaviour (observer) reveal many situational explanations. The actor–observer difference can be reduced or reversed by using strategies that make dispositions more salient for the actor, and situational factors more salient for the observer. This is summarised in Figure 3.4.

Overall, considerable evidence, from laboratory experiments and more naturalistic studies, shows the traditional actor–observer differences to be a consistent effect under many conditions. However, this should not be taken to mean that actors exclusively make situational attributions, and observers make exclusively dispositional attributions. They do not. We have also seen that the orientation, to take just one factor, of the observer can reverse the effect.

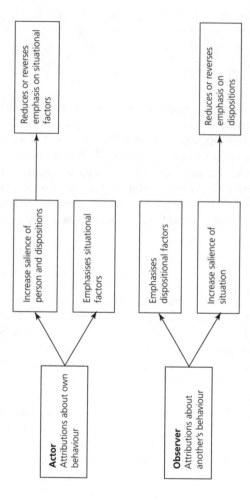

Figure 3.4 **Actor–observer differences in causal explanations and effects of increasing salience of under-emphasised factors**

The false consensus effect

Imagine that you have recently been asked to give up your Saturday to do community work for Help the Aged. This requires you to weed the beds and mow the grass of the gardens of elderly people who live at home but are unable to cope with such tasks. You agree to do these tasks. Then you wonder to yourself how many of your friends would have also agreed to give up their Saturday in such a way. You assume that most have. Later you find that only one or two have agreed to volunteer for the community work and you feel surprised by this. This example demonstrates the **false consensus effect** which is the tendency for people to overestimate how common their own behaviour, beliefs, attitudes, etc. are amongst other people.

The false consensus effect was demonstrated in a classic study by Ross *et al.* (1977). Here college students were asked to walk around their campus wearing a large sandwich board advertising 'Eat at Joe's'. Some students agreed to take part whilst others refused. Those who agreed were then asked to estimate how many of their fellow students would also agree to this request. The estimate they gave was 62 per cent. By contrast those who refused estimated that 67 per cent of their fellow students would also refuse! Ross *et al.* actually found that of the 80 college students asked 48 agreed (60 per cent) and 32 refused (40 per cent). A large number of studies show the false consensus effect to be robust and replicable across a wide range of behaviours, attitudes and opinions (Marks and Miller, 1987).

Three main explanations have been offered for the false consensus effect. First, our friends and intimate partner may be among people who are likely to be similar to us. Due to the fact that most of our social interaction takes place with our friends/partner, who by and large have similar views to us, we take these shared views to exist more commonly amongst people we do not know, than they actually are. Second, our own attitudes, opinions and beliefs will be highly salient and at the forefront of our mind. When we come across people expressing similar attitudes, we may focus on this and believe the attitude is commonly held amongst many people. This leads to an overestimation of how commonly held the attitude is with other people. Third, motivation and our own self-esteem may have a role to play in that our own self-esteem may be enhanced by believing that other people hold the same opinions as ourselves. This may provide validity and bolster confidence in our own views with the result that we see ourselves as 'right' to hold such views. It seems then, that a mixture of cognitive and motivational explanations account for the false consensus effect.

With over 20 years of research social psychologists have identified a number of factors which may enhance or reduce the effect (Fiske and Taylor, 1991). False consensus effects are stronger when:

- the behaviour is seen to directly result from strong situational influences
- when the matter is of great importance to the person
- when we have a high degree of confidence that our view is correct or accurate

False consensus effects are weak or not in evidence when:

- a person has no idea about how others might behave in a certain situation
- when negative qualities or attributes about ourselves are involved
- when we actually do share a view held by a high majority of people

In our consideration of the false consensus effect there has been an implicit assumption that it is a bias or error. Dawes (1989) has argued to the contrary that the effect may be a rational strategy since it may make sense to assume that our behaviour and/or views are common amongst other people. In the absence of other information, evidence or alternative strategies the generalisation may be justified.

Self-serving biases

You have just attended an interview for a job that you would very much like to have, you thought the interview went well and that you gave a good account of yourself. A couple of days later you are contacted and told that you have the job. It is most likely that you will attribute your success to internal dispositions such as ability, effort and good interpersonal skills. Imagine on the other hand that you did not get the job. Because you wanted it so much attributions to external and situational factors, such as noisy room, rude interviewer or irrelevant questions asked, may be made. This pattern of attributions for success and failure is what is known as the **self-serving bias**. This may be defined as 'the tendency to take credit for success and deny responsibility for failure' (Fiske and Taylor, 1991).

Evidence for such an attributional bias came from an early study by Johnson *et al.* (1964). In this experiment students were asked to teach secondary school pupils mathematics. The students were told that after their teaching, one pupil had performed well and one poorly. The students were then required to teach more mathematics to each pupil. Following this the student teachers were told that:

- the pupil who had done well following their first teaching session had continued to do well
- the pupil who had done poorly the first time had *either* continued to do poorly *or* improved

The student teachers were then asked to provide causal explanations for the pupil's performances. It was found that improved performance in the poor pupil was attributed to internal dispositions such as their own teaching skills and knowledge of mathematics. In contrast, for pupils who continued to do poorly the student teachers made external attributions such as pupil's lack of effort and inability to grasp mathematics.

Research over twenty years has found this self-serving bias to be a robust effect which is supported by cross-cultural research (Fletcher and Ward, 1988). Generally, empirical evidence has found stronger support for people taking credit for success (called a **self-enhancing bias**) than for people not accepting responsibility for failure (called a **self-protective bias**). The two types of bias within the general self-serving bias are shown in Figure 3.5.

Two types of explanation have been offered to explain self-serving biases – cognitive and motivational factors (Fiske and Taylor, 1991). Motivational explanations are based on the idea that the ego needs to protect itself from harm and present yourself to other people in the best light. Hence, the ego defends itself by taking credit for success and blaming others for failure. Cognitive explanations are based around expectations that people have: you expect or hope to succeed at tasks you set yourself. For example, a boxer going into the ring before a fight will do his best to convince himself that he is a better boxer and will win. This may, in part, be due to people believing their own success

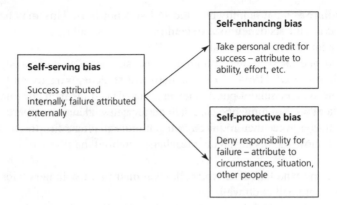

Figure 3.5 **How the self-serving bias may result in either self-enhancement or self-protective biases**

is under their control – but note our consideration of personality differences in Chapter 2 and the attributional style of depressives.

Evaluation

Some limiting factors for the generality of self-serving biases have been identified. For example, when there is public acclaim for personal success, such as that following an heroic deed, modesty and a tendency to give external explanations may be self-serving (Schlenker *et al.*, 1990). Also, if someone knows that their future performance will be critically examined there may be a tendency not to take so much credit for success (Miller and Schlenko, 1985).

Generally, research reports that people take more credit for success, whilst the evidence is less consistent for people denying personal responsibility for failure. The self-serving bias has also been found to be reduced when an act of behaviour comes under public scrutiny (such as a public enquiry or court case), and reversed sometimes when a person is trying to appear modest (Taylor and Fiske, 1991).

Group bias

Up to now we have considered self-serving biases at an individual level. However, Hewstone (1989) has identified a counterpart operating at the group level which is called the **group-serving attributional bias** or **ethnocentric bias**.

To understand this, think about a social or sports group that you are a member of. This may be a football or hockey team, or a self-help psychology group to deal with statistics! The group you identify yourself as a member of is called the ingroup, and other groups of which you are not a member are called outgroups. Hewstone (1989) found that if your own group did well on a task – for example, the group you played hockey with won their match – then dispositional attributions tend to be made. Here this might be such things as how well you all work as a team, the high level of skills of each person in the team, etc. By contrast, your attributions to the team you played against and who lost (negative behaviour) will tend to be situational (poorly trained, not used to playing away, etc.). This differential pattern of attributions serves the function of enhancing the positive aspects of the group you belong to, and making the other group look weaker or more ineffective than they actually are. In Chapter 5 we will look in much more detail into ingroup–outgroup effects. Figure 3.6 provides another example of this group-serving attributional bias.

List each of the three attributional errors/biases that we have considered and identify the conditions under which each occurs. Then list the factors that have been found to reduce or reverse the error/bias.

Review exercise

Attributions of responsibility

Driving accidents are all too common on our roads, and after an accident happens both the police and insurance companies are interested in who is responsible and to blame for the accident. This is especially so when the accident is serious and causes severe personal injury or even death. Broadly speaking, internal or dispositional attributions result in a person being held responsible, whilst external attributions place the responsibility elsewhere. Shaver (1985) provides

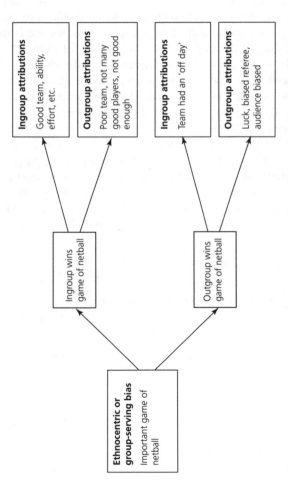

Ethnocentric or group-serving bias

Important game of netball

Ingroup wins game of netball

Ingroup attributions

Good team, ability, effort, etc.

Outgroup attributions

Poor team, not many good players, not good enough

Outgroup wins game of netball

Ingroup attributions

Team had an 'off day'

Outgroup attributions

Luck, biased referee, audience biased

Figure 3.6 The ethnocentric or group-serving bias shown through attributions made by the ingroup following the outcome of an important game of netball

a theoretical framework for understanding how responsibility and blame is attributed. Four factors are involved: there has to be a person identifiable as the originator of the behaviour; a belief that the person should have been able to foresee the outcome of his or her behaviour; a perception that the behaviour was not justified; and the person had free choice. Figure 3.7 summarises this and uses an example of a motor car accident to highlight these factors.

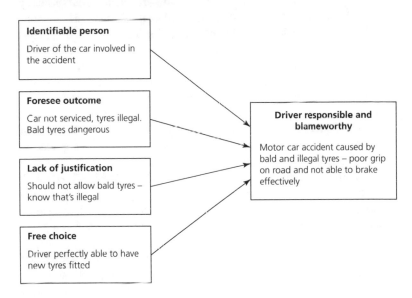

Figure 3.7 **Use of example of motor car accident to exemplify Shaver's (1985) framework for attributing blame**

Defensive attributional biases have been identified from research on attributions of responsibility. It has generally been found that behaviours resulting in severe outcomes (motor accident resulting in death, for example) attract greater levels of responsibility to the person involved than when outcomes are minor (motor accident resulting in broken headlight). As an outcome of behaviour becomes more severe the idea that the consequence was accidental (external attribution) becomes less acceptable to people and internal causes identifying responsibility are sought. Generally, the more unpleasant, undesirable and upsetting the outcome, the greater the defensive attributional bias to ascribing responsibility and blame.

People exhibit a defensive attributional bias if a high degree of personal similarity is perceived between the person responsible for the outcome and the observer. For example, suppose a doctor refuses to treat an alcoholic for a condition that is a direct consequence of excessive and regular drinking. You read about this in the newspaper and being a teetotaller yourself agree with the doctor and attribute responsibility for the condition to the alcoholic's inability to control his or her drinking. However, suppose you are an alcoholic or heavy drinker yourself. Burger (1981) showed that less personal responsibility will be attributed to the alcoholic for his or her medical condition. This is a defensive attribution since you are seeking to deny to yourself responsibility for the consequences of heavy drinking. Thornton (1984) generalised this idea to suggest that the higher the perceived personal threat, the more defensive attributions will be present.

In Chapter 2 we examined Weiner's (1979, 1986) model of attributions for success and failure. This model has good application for helping us to understand responsibility and blame in respect of such social problems as poverty, murder and rape (Lord, 1997). Clearly with crimes such as rape or murder the legal system is crucially concerned about attributing responsibility for the behaviour – this will determine both guilt and the severity of sentence passed on the person convicted of the crime.

Let us consider poverty in this context. Using Weiner's model, if we were to attribute a person's poverty to internal, stable and controllable causes the consequence would be that the person would be held responsible for the poverty he or she finds themselves in. By contrast, if a person's poverty is attributed to external, unstable and uncontrollable causes the person would not be held responsible and would receive both our help and sympathy. Zucker and Weiner (1993) produced evidence that a person's political leanings moderated this general assertion. They found that conservatives in the United States thought that poor people were more personally responsible for their plight and could do more to avoid poverty than liberals. Skitka and Tetlock (1993) suggest that conservatives are more likely to attribute internal, stable and controllable causes to people who find themselves poor, contract AIDS and other medical conditions. United States liberals look more to external, unstable causes for similar or social problems. On the face of it this should parallel conservative and labour voters in this country and this has been supported in research by Furnham (1982).

Overall, good support has been found for the idea that less responsibility is attributed to another person when we see ourselves as similar to that person in terms of attitudes, beliefs, and personality. This no doubt underestimates the other person's responsibility and results from defensiveness on our part. Crudely speaking, if we perceive ourselves to be similar to another person we find it threatening to think they can do bad things. To do so would imply that we could do bad things also.

Cross-cultural perspectives on bias and error

In Chapter 2 we considered research investigating cultural differences in relation to internal and external attributions and saw that 'individualist' or 'independent' cultures showed a greater tendency towards making internal or dispositional attributions and 'collectivist' or 'interdependent' cultures showed a tendency towards external or situational attributions. This has relevance in relation to the extent that the fundamental attribution error may be prevalent across cultures. On the basis of what has just been said we would not expect it to be so. This is supported by Newman (1993) who claims that collectivist cultures are less likely to make dispositional or spontaneous internal attributions. For example, Hindus in India are more likely to refer to other people when explaining behaviour (her friends supported her) rather than dispositional explanation (she is a kind person). Research by Morris and Peng (1994), detailed in Chapter 2, supports the assertion that the fundamental attribution error is more a feature of western, individualistic cultures than collectivist cultures such as China (Krull and Erickson, 1995). Miller (1984) investigated the prevalence or frequency of dispositional attributions made by children or young adults in North American and Indian Hindu cultures. Participants were asked to give causal explanations for both pro-social and anti-social behaviours. A free-response format was used to avoid imposing a North American approach and these were then analysed for the presence of dispositional attributions.

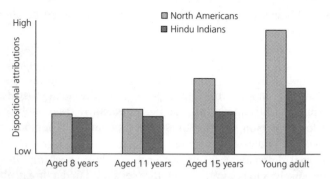

Figure 3.8 **Dispositional attributions made by North Americans and Hindu Indians from 8 years of age to young adulthood**
Source: After Miller, 1984

As Figure 3.8 shows, the proportion of dispositional attributions shown by 8 year-olds from both cultures was similar and, interestingly, quite low. However, with increase in age the two groups diverged with North Americans showing higher levels of dispositional attributions as they became adults. Miller (1984) also analysed external or situational attributions for the same free-responses and found the opposite. That is, Hindu Indians showed more such attributions as they became adults, whilst North Americans did not. Clearly this research supports the idea that the type of culture plays a strong role in determining the attributions (dispositional or situational) that people make. Given all this, the question now becomes how frequently other attributional biases occur across cultures. This will be looked at in terms of the self-serving bias.

Kashima and Triandis (1986) found evidence for the opposite of a self-serving bias in Japanese students, which they called a self-effacement or modesty bias. In this study American and Japanese students were asked, using a free-response format, to explain their successes and failures at academic study. The traditional self-serving bias was present in American students but not in Japanese students. Japanese students attributed failures more to personal characteristics such as ability than they did their successes. The reverse, as you might expect, was true for the American students. Earlier research by Fry and Ghosh (1980), using children between the ages of 8 and 10 years from white Canadian and Asian Indian Canadian groups, found similar attribution patterns. For example, Asian Indian Canadians attributed success more to luck, and failure more to lack of ability, while white Canadians showed the opposite pattern.

The conclusion we may draw from these cross-cultural studies is that attributional errors and biases do not seem to be consistent across cultures. Individualistic cultures tend to foster the fundamental attribution error, in contrast collectivist cultures display the opposite to a self-serving bias in the form of a self-effacement bias. Bias and error occur across cultures but they are different in nature.

Evaluation of attributional biases and errors

At the start of this chapter the issue of how we judge accuracy and error in relation to attributions was raised. From the different biases and errors considered in this chapter, together with supporting research, it is fair to criticise social psychologists for being too keen to look for error and less concerned with accuracy. For example, when do you *really know* if someone convicted of manslaughter (as with our imaginary scenario of a wife killing her husband) did not plan the act in advance (and hence make it murder?). Very little, if any, of the literature in the attribution approach considers this. Yet it is apparent that our explanations of causes for behaviour in everyday life serve us well enough to live, adjust, and interact effectively with other people. Our justice system is built on how we validate judgements of responsibility and blame. Our legal system works quite effectively the vast majority of the time, but does succumb to dreadful miscarriages of justice at other times. In the end, because we are considering people's thoughts and thought processes we are never really going to have an entirely objective way of stating whether an attribution is accurate or in error.

The errors and biases that we have looked at in this chapter do not seem to generalise across different cultures, particularly in relation to individualistic and collectivist cultures. Furthermore, some of these biases and errors are more likely to be seen in paper and pencil type tasks (Fiske and Taylor, 1991) than in real-life situations. In view of this it is open to question just how much they may be artefacts of the social psychology experiment rather than actually occurring in everyday life. More research is needed on this matter.

The internal–external distinction is fundamental to understanding biases and errors. However, the distinction is not as clear cut as might appear on first acquaintance. Ross (1977) draws our attention to this by asking us to think of a simple example concerning why somebody buys a house in a particular location. The person might justify their choice of house by saying it is secluded (external attribution) and this caused the person to buy it. However, you would only buy a secluded house if you valued privacy highly (an internal attribution). Hence, couching an explanation as an internal attribution does also allow external considerations!

Finally, the focus on biases and errors in the attribution process emphasises both an individual and cognitive perspective. This may result in a tendency to exaggerate the extent to which people seek to make causal attributions for behaviour. Nevertheless, the attribution approach and the study of errors and biases is both an important and influential area in social psychology. It is also one which has enjoyed numerous valuable applications as we shall see later in this book. In Chapter 6 we consider two applications of the attribution approach – sport and health. You may wish to dip into one or both of these now.

Summary

The way people actually make attributions deviates from the models considered in Chapter 2, and reveals that numerous errors and bias are present in our everyday causal attributions. The fundamental attribution error is the widespread tendency for people to overestimate the importance of dispositions and neglect situational or external causes of behaviour. The fundamental attribution error may result from both behaviour engulfing our perceptual field and from spontaneous rather than deliberate thought.

Actor–observer differences are present when explaining your own behaviour (actor) situational or external causes are emphasised, and when explaining another's behaviour internal or dispositional causes are emphasised. The false consensus effect is where people overestimate how common their own behaviour, beliefs, and opinions are amongst other people. Self-serving biases are where you make internal attributions for success and external attributions for failure: the former is self-enhancing and the latter self-protecting. Self-serving biases result from both cognitive and motivational factors, the latter being to do with ego-defensiveness. Attributions of responsibility and blame relate to Weiner's model of success and failure. Internal attributions lead to people being held responsible for their actions.

Cross-cultural research comparing individualistic versus collectivist cultures shows that the fundamental attribution error and the self-serving bias may occur more in the former culture. In collectivist cultures there is evidence for a self-effacement bias. Social psychologists have focused too much attention on error and bias and not enough on accuracy in causal explanation. The internal–external distinction may not be a clear cut difference on which to base attributions.

Further reading

Augostinos, M. and Walker, I. (1995) *Social Cognition: an Integrated Approach*, London: Sage Publications.

Provides good coverage of the various attributional biases and errors together with a critical commentary. Later chapters attempt to integrate North American and European social psychology traditions to provide an integration. Readable and offers interesting perspectives.

Fiske, S. T. and Taylor, S. E. (1991) *Social Cognition*, 2nd edn, New York: McGraw-Hill.

Offers just the same level of detail in relation to attributional errors and biases as for models and approaches to how we attribute causes. Advanced text but readable all the same.

Weiner, B. (1995) *Judgements of Responsibility*, New York: Guildford.

Advanced text which updates and develops Weiner's earlier theoretical approach to explaining success and failure and develops it in the context of how we make causal attributions resulting in judgements of responsibility.

4

Social perception
Impression formation, social schemas and social representations

What is social perception?

You have applied for a job that you very much want and have been invited for interview. You decide that the correct thing to do is wear smart clothes and present yourself as having good interpersonal skills. Although nervous at interview you do your best to smile and convey the impression that you are likeable and hence easy to work with, whilst at the same time diligent and hard working.

A friend of yours introduces you to somebody you have never met before. Your friend tells you that this person is a member of the environmental pressure group Greenpeace. Before meeting the person you expect him to hold socialist attitudes, favour organic food and be against genetically modified food. You also expect him to wear jeans, t-shirt and sandals.

You have a new psychology teacher who will shortly be taking you for classes. A friend of yours at another college has told you that she was taught by this person and that he is a good teacher whom it is easy to relate to. This psychology teacher is also, according to your friend, very enthusiastic about psychology, a warm person, but with a tendency to be arrogant at times. From this description you find yourself greatly looking forward to being taught psychology by this person.

These three examples have a number of things in common: first, they are all related to **social perception** and **impression formation**. Second, each demonstrates the importance of first impressions, whether from actual experience or what you have been told about another person. Finally, each emphasises how expectations may influence what you say and do, as well as how your impression of a person might partly be formed before you have ever actually met him or her.

Social perception may broadly be defined as 'the process through which we seek to know and understand other persons' (Baron and Byrne, 2000). In a sense then, social perception may be used interchangeably with social cognition, since the above definition encompasses all the different topics covered in the chapters in this book. However, for the purposes of this chapter we will take social perception to be about impression formation, social schemas and social representations, Social perception is commonly linked to the term **stereotypes**, and this is dealt with in some detail in Chapter 5 where stereotype is usually considered in the context of prejudice and discrimination.

Impression formation

Theory and research in psychology on impression formation has centred around how we form first impressions of another person, how enduring such first impressions are, and how we can attempt to manage the impression others form of us. In what follows we shall look at each of these aspects of impression formation.

The importance of first impressions

Imagine yourself in the position of being interviewed for a job, like our example at the start of this chapter. How you dress, the way you sit when responding to questions, and how you smile and look at the interviewer can all have powerful effects on the first impression that is formed of you. Research has shown that superficial clues, such as those above, do influence the first impression formed (Bull and Rumsey, 1988). The actual configuration of your face, something largely beyond your control unless you have plastic surgery, can affect the first impression. For example, adults with a 'baby face' – large eyes, and small nose relative to the rest of the face – may be perceived as more naïve, honest and kind, but also as submissive, socially incompetent and powerless (Zebrowitz, 1990). People we judge as very attractive are generally perceived as interesting, warm, outgoing and socially skilled (Feingold, 1992), such traits are regarded as central to impression formation and hence exert a high degree of influence.

> Find a friend to work with and conduct a mock interview (for example, as if you are being considered for a university place). Interview each other twice; once where you try to act as normal and once where you have your body turned away from your friend and do not look him or her in the face or eyes. Consider the different impressions conveyed from both interviews with your friend.

Progress exercise

Central and peripheral traits

Theory and research on impression formation dates back over 50 years to the pioneering work of Solomon Asch (1946). Asch argued that an impression is a dynamic product of all the information available to the person forming the impression. However, some information is of greater importance and influence than other information. Asch demonstrated this in a classic and key experiment in which participants were presented with one of two lists of trait descriptions as follows:

List 1: intelligent, skilful, industrious, warm, determined, practical, cautious

List 2: intelligent, skilful, industrious, cold, determined, practical, cautious

Participants were given one of these two lists and subsequently asked to write a brief sketch of the person and rate impressions on a different set of trait descriptors. Notice that the only difference between the two lists given above are the adjectives *warm* and *cold*. Asch (1946) found that participants given List 1 rated the hypothetical person as generous, happy, good-natured and humane, whilst those given List 2 rated the imaginary person as ungenerous, unhappy, humourless and ruthless.

Asch concluded that for just one trait dimension – warm/cold – to have such a dramatic effect must mean that warm/cold is a **central trait** which influences many other trait descriptors of a person. To check this Asch conducted a series of further experiments using similar trait lists but varying just one trait dimension, for example:

List 3: intelligent, skilful, industrious, *polite*, determined, practical, cautious

List 4: intelligent, skilful, industrious, *blunt*, determined, practical, cautious

The only difference between Lists 1/2 and Lists 3/4 is the substitution of warm/cold for polite/blunt. Asch found no difference in the sketch and ratings given by participants after reading either List 3 or 4. Hence, Asch concluded that polite/blunt are **peripheral traits**, which have little influence over the impression formed.

Evaluation

One of the main criticisms of Asch's research is that the participants were asked to think of an imaginary person rather than basing their impression on experience of a real person. Kelley (1950) sought to overcome this by presenting psychology students with a guest lecturer. Prior to the students having the lecture they were provided with a description of him. Half of the students received the following description:

> Mr Smith is a graduate student in the Department of Economics and Social Science. He has had three semesters of teaching experience in psychology in another college. This is his first semester teaching Economics here. He is 26 years old, a veteran, and married. People who know him consider him to be rather a *cold* person, industrious, critical, practical and determined.

The other half of the students received exactly the same outline but with the word *warm* substituted for cold. The guest lecturer then gave a 20 minute lecture and after he had left, students were asked to give their impressions of him. Kelley's findings supported those of Asch. Additionally, Kelley found that students interacted with and asked more questions of the lecturer who was described as warm. Kelley's research has the advantages over Asch's of being more realistic and allowing students to interact with the lecturer. However, both sets of research only deal with impression formation in the context of limited contact and information about a person over a short period of time. Also, no further encounter, real or imagined, takes place, i.e. a relationship with the person does not develop.

Implicit personality theory

On the basis of the above research and many other studies demonstrating the idea of central and peripheral traits, Asch stated that:

> There is an attempt to form an impression of the entire person. As soon as two or more traits are perceived to belong to the one person they cease to exist as isolated traits.
>
> (Asch, 1946)

This conceptualisation led Bruner and Taguiri (1954) to propose that people possess **implicit personality theories**. An implicit personality theory is a general expectation that an individual has about a person resulting from knowledge about central traits. Implicit personality theory implies that people hold preconceptions about what an individual is like, on a broad front and encompassing the entire individual, based on knowledge of just a few central traits. How we form an implicit personality theory about others is largely culturally and socially based (Schneider, 1973).

Primacy and recency effects

Look back to the example at the start of this chapter – we all regard first impressions as vital when attending a job interview. First impressions made may be seen as a **primacy effect**; this is where information about another person which is present first has greater influence on the impression formed than information which comes later. The reverse is a **recency effect**; this is where information presented last has the greatest influence on the impression formed.

A classic experiment by Luchins (1957) demonstrated both the primacy effect and conditions most likely to result in a recency effect. Luchins (1957) presented participants with two paragraphs about a person named Jim. Having read the two paragraphs, participants were then asked to write their impressions of him. One paragraph described Jim as friendly, outgoing and extrovert. This paragraph reads as follows:

> Jim left the house to get some stationery. He walked out into the sun-filled street with two of his friends, basking in the sun as he walked. Jim entered the stationery store which was full of people. Jim talked with an acquaintance while he waited for the clerk to catch his eye. On his way out he stopped to chat to a school friend who was just coming out of the store. Leaving the store, he walked towards school. On his way out he met a girl to whom he had been introduced the night before. They talked for a short while, and then Jim left for school.

The second paragraph described Jim as shy, reclusive and introvert.

This paragraph reads as follows:

> After school Jim left the classroom alone. Leaving the school, he started on his long walk home. The street was brilliantly filled with sunshine. Jim walked down the shady side of the street. Coming down the street towards him he saw the pretty girl whom he had met the previous evening. Jim crossed the street and entered the candy store. The store was crowded with students, and he noticed a few familiar faces. Jim waited quietly until the shop assistant caught his eye, and then gave his order. Taking his drink, he sat down at a side table. When he had finished his drink he went home.
>
> (Luchins, 1957, p. 35)

Half the participants read the extrovert paragraph followed by the introvert paragraph, the other half read the paragraphs in the reverse order. Luchins found a primacy effect when the two paragraphs were read in immediate succession. A recency effect occurred when there was a time delay of 15 minutes between reading the two paragraphs. Research shows that primacy effects are more common than recency effects (McKelvie, 1990). This is probably because information presented first is assimilated rapidly into a person schema (see the section on page 71). The person schema becomes established and is consequently more difficult to change to accommodate information presented later.

Evaluation

This early experiment of Luchins (1957) suffers similar shortcomings to those of Asch (1946) in that the material presented to participants is artificial; participants do not actually see a real person, and no further engagement with the imagined person takes place. Additionally, little account is taken of participants' existing ideas of people (or stereotypes). Hence it seems that an impression is formed in a vacuum when in fact each person brings a range of social schemas (especially person schemas) with them and prior to receiving information about somebody they do not know. In the sections on pages 69–79 we shall explore social schemas more fully and you will see how they offer a richer and fuller understanding of person perception and impression formation.

Look back to what has been said about central and peripheral traits. Take one or two examples of each and construct short paragraphs similar to those of Luchins. Do you think central traits are more likely to produce primary effects than peripheral traits, or do you think both types of traits will produce primacy effects? Justify your answer.

Impression management

When you attend for an interview you will no doubt try your very hardest to create a favourable impression of yourself. In effect what you try to do is make efforts at **impression management**. Social psychologists have identified two broad techniques that people commonly use: self-enhancement and other-enhancement. *Self-enhancement* may include paying careful attention to how you dress, describing yourself in positive ways and appearing more intelligent, for example, by wearing glasses. For example, Rowatt *et al.* (1998) found that people using self-enhancement techniques when trying to make a date with a person are more successful than people who are more self-effacing and honest about themselves.

Other-enhancement methods of impression management are techniques which attempt to make the other person feel good. The most obvious example is flattery, but this should not be overdone. Other techniques include agreeing with the other person, appearing to be very interested in what the other person has to say, and asking for their advice over matters.

If you are going consciously to attempt to manage the impression of yourself to another person, one golden rule is not to overdo self-enhancement or other-enhancement techniques. Using both together at the same time is effective, but overdone you may create a negative impression of yourself instead (Baron and Byrne, 2000).

Accuracy in social perception

An impression of a person is just that – there is no guarantee that the impression formed is an accurate reflection of how the person really is. This is especially the case if the other person is actively trying to manage the impression you are gaining of them. The question needs to be asked, then, about how we might determine how accurate we can be in social perception. Kenny (1991) suggests three main ways in which an assessment of accuracy in social perception may be made. These are: agreeing with self-reports; agreeing with others; and predicting future behaviour. *Agreeing with self-reports* is where two people, one of whom an impression is formed, actually agree between them on the personality traits, attitudes, etc. of one of them. *Agreeing with others* is where a number of other people agree with the person who has formed an impression of the target person. *Predicting future behaviour*, perhaps the most useful measure, is where the impression formed leads to accurate prediction of what the person will actually do. The latter may be regarded as the most useful since behaviour can be readily observed and more objectively measured than a personality trait. Research has also shown that people tend to be more accurate in their perception of central traits, such as extroversion, than other traits which are peripheral (Levesque and Kenny, 1993).

Social schemas

You and your partner have decided to eat out and have booked a table at a good restaurant. Upon arrival at the restaurant you are ushered to a seated waiting area. As you sit there you mentally run through ordering your food, being escorted to the table, having wine served and poured into your glass. This all brings a smile to your face since you expect to enjoy the evening greatly.

This common social episode exemplifies the concept of **social schemas**. Social schemas may be defined as cognitive structures which represent 'knowledge about a concept or type of stimulus, including its attributes and relations among those attributes' (Fiske and Taylor, 1991, p. 98). Put another way social schemas are organised collections of information stored in memory and based on past experience. Schemas offer shorthand summaries of our social world and enable us readily and easily to code and categorise new information, rather than starting from a blank sheet every time we encounter a different social situation.

Schemas facilitate and may determine encoding of new information. For example, schemas influence what to pay attention to and what to ignore; usually information consistent with a schema is stored in memory and inconsistent information ignored or forgotten. Schemas help us to process information quickly. Schemas also influence what we remember about a social situation and may cause us to go beyond the information given when trying to recall details of an incident. Cohen (1981) showed two groups of participants the same video of a woman eating a meal. One group was told she was a librarian and the other group that she was a waitress. Those in the former condition recalled that she wore glasses and said she liked classical music; those in the latter condition, that she was drinking a beer and was watching television. Social schemas, then, can both affect the impression we form of people and what we remember about them; in effect, they are a development of implicit personality theory (see pages 65–6). As can be seen from the above study, erroneous claims to what is remembered may be a consequence of social schemas. In the language of cognitive psychology, schemas offer a 'top down' approach to information processing as opposed to a 'bottom up' approach which is driven by the data without preconceived frameworks such as schemas. Figure 4.1 summarises the key features of schemas we have considered so far.

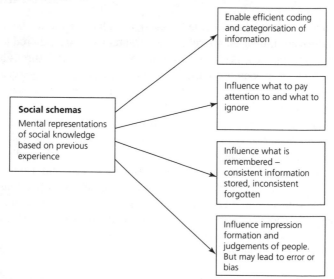

Figure 4.1 **Key features of the role social schemas play in social cognition**

Social psychologists have identified numerous groups or clusters of schemas, the main ones being: person schemas, self-schemas, role schemas, and event schemas. In what follows we shall look at these four schemas.

Person schemas

As you come to know somebody through social interaction, reading about them, hearing their music, listening to what their friends have to say, you build up a **person schema**. A schema for 'your best friend', for example, might include expected behaviours and personality traits together with certain attitudes and beliefs. Over the time you have known your best friend you have built up quite a detailed person schema for him or her. This serves to provide you with expectations about your friend's future behaviour and to make judgements about continuing the friendship. Notice that such a person schema is related to a particular individual. People also have schemas which represent ideal or perfect types – these are called **prototypes**. A prototypical best friend is a schema that represents all the ideal attributes (personality, beliefs, attitudes, interests, etc.) that you think a best friend should possess. When the person schema of your actual best friend has a lot in common with your prototypical best friend that person will stay your best friend. However, should your best friend change and develop new interests and different attitudes from yours, the gap between prototype and person schema will grow and you may decide that he or she is becoming too different for you to maintain such a close friendship. Prototypes have a lot in common with stereotypes and as such may lead to prejudice and discrimination (see Chapter 5).

Think of three or four people you regard as good friends and try to identify similarities – traits, attitudes, dress, etc. – between them. List these and you will have developed, in part, your prototype of a 'friend'.

Progress exercise

Self-schemas

Self-schemas are defined by Markus (1977) as 'cognitive general-isations about the self, derived from past experience, that organise and guide the processing of self-related information'. Markus (1977) coined the term 'schematic' to apply to traits, attitudes, etc. that are of central importance to a person, and 'aschematic' where such features are of peripheral or minor importance. For example, a person who finds it important to and likes to spend a lot of time with other people will be schematic on the trait of gregariousness. By contrast, a person who is not interested in sport will be aschematic for sport. Notice that being schematic for a trait, attitude, etc. means that the trait etc. is important to you and this can be in either a positive or negative manner. Wurf and Markus (1983) produced evidence that negative aschematic traits result in people quickly identifying what they are *not*, but schematic traits do not result in quick identification of what you *are* like. The concepts of schematic and aschematic do presuppose that people know themselves and know what they are like. Markus and Nurius (1986) introduce the idea of **possible selves** to recognise the fact that we use goals, roles and ambitions to which we aspire in the future. Possible selves act as guides to information we need, behaviours and attitudes to make happen the desired future objective. In general, possible selves are self-schemas about how we would like to be and serve important motivational functions.

Role schemas

Look back to the examples given at the start of this chapter. How you approach the interview may be seen to be how you take on the role of interviewee. As such **role schemas** are 'the set of behaviours expected of a person in a particular social situation' (Fiske and Taylor, 1991, p. 119). People have a large number of role schemas mentally repre-sented; these include, for example, the roles of student, husband/wife, waiter, policeman, father/mother. Clearly there are too many to enumerate here.

A distinction is made between **ascribed** and **achieved** roles. Achieved roles are those a person has actually managed to acquire such as teacher, salesman, professor, etc. When a person achieves a role others may have quite strong expectations, from their own role schemas, of how the role should be enacted. Behavioural deviations from the expected enactment of a role may cause the person problems; for example, a policeman who accepts bribes and is corrupted or a teacher who is unfair to a particular pupil. Ascribed roles are ones that you acquire automatically because of birth or sex or age or race. You cannot do much about ascribed roles. For example, if you are the son or daughter of the Queen of England there are numerous ascribed roles attached. Again the role schemas held by other people put social pressure on people to behave consistently with the ascribed role. Sex, race, age, and disability stereotypes are negative consequences of ascribed role schemas.

Identify your own goals and ambitions in life – these will be role schemes of possible selves. Identify two ascribed and two achieved roles for yourself. Relate these to role schemas.

Progress exercise

Event schemas

The scenario of going out to eat given at the start of this section is an example of an **event schema** or **script** (Schank and Abelson, 1977). Event schemas or scripts are mental representations of what we normally expect in a multitude of social situations. Hence, we have scripts for restaurants, interviews, behaviour in class, parties, going to the pub, going to the theatre or cinema, etc. Figure 4.2 depicts details of an event schema that applies to eating out in a restaurant.

Event schemas bring both sense and richness of understanding to a film we watch or story we read. In general, event scripts provide people with expectations about a sequence of events in particular social situations.

Summary

The four types of schemas we have considered should not be regarded as distinctive or, more importantly, entirely separate from each other.

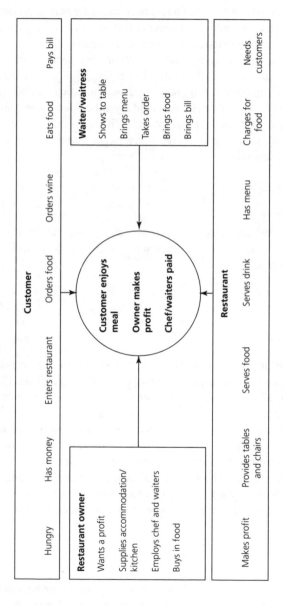

Customer

| Hungry | Has money | Enters restaurant | Orders food | Orders wine | Eats food | Pays bill |

Customer enjoys meal

Owner makes profit

Chef/waiters paid

Restaurant owner

Wants a profit

Supplies accommodation/ kitchen

Employs chef and waiters

Buys in food

Waiter/waitress

Shows to table

Brings menu

Takes order

Brings food

Brings bill

Restaurant

| Makes profit | Provides tables and chairs | Serves food | Serves drink | Has menu | Charges for food | Needs customers |

Figure 4.2 **Event schemas or script for eating out in a restaurant**

We have seen, using the example of the interview, how role schemas influence the behaviour of the interviewee and event schemas determine what you can expect to happen at interview. Figure 4.3 summarises the main features of these four schemas.

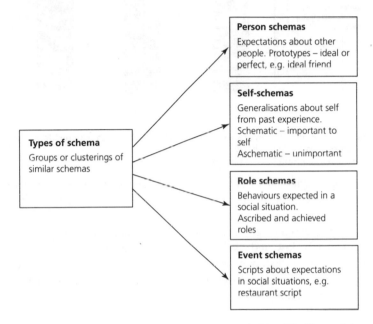

Figure 4.3 Four types of schema most commonly identified by social psychologists

Schemas that have become established and developed from a great deal of experience may be quite resistant to change with pressure to maintain the status quo (Fiske and Taylor, 1991). An early demonstration of how we resist change once a self-schema has been established was given by Ross, Lepper and Hubbard (1975). This study was conducted to examine **belief perseverance** – the maintenance of beliefs in the face of *dis*confirming evidence. Ross, Lepper and Hubbard (1975) asked participants to look at two suicide notes and decide which was fake and which real. One third of the participants were led to believe they had guessed correctly on 24 of the 25 trials, another third 17 correct from 25 and the final third 10 correct of the 25. Ross and his colleagues then told participants this feedback was

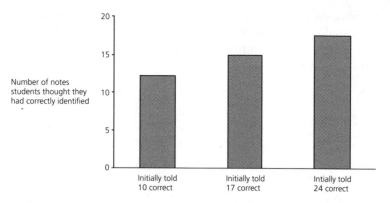

Figure 4.4 Belief perseverance after initial feedback about suicide note judgements was discredited
Source: **Adapted from Ross, Lepper and Hubbard, 1975**

made up. Participants were then asked to guess how many they had actually correctly identified. As Figure 4.4 shows, even when the initial feedback was discredited belief perseverance was in evidence.

Other research on schema change and resistance to change shows that change is slow, and results from many instances of discriminating evidence (rather than one). Also, as schemas become more complex they may develop into sub-schemas or split into two or more separate schemas (Rothbart, 1981).

Social schemas as stereotypes

Stereotypes may be regarded as more generalised social schemas, particularly role schemas. Chapter 5 explores stereotypes more fully in relation to prejudice and discrimination. Anderson and Klatzky (1987) distinguish between social schemas and stereotypes by saying that the latter are more complex, well-established, and likely to be more culturally determined than either role or person schemas. Person schemas especially are more likely to be related to individual characteristics, whilst stereotypes are where individual characteristics are ignored and a person is assumed to hold attitudes and possess personality traits of a typical member of the relevant social category. Nevertheless, there is a temptation to use social schemas and stereotypes interchangeably. One important and far-reaching difference to keep in mind is that stereotypes are often negative and reflect prejudicial attitudes. By contrast, the four types of social schema do not necessarily have these connotations.

Social schemas and impression formation

Recall our coverage of impression formation on pages 62–9. You may see that it is possible to interpret this work in terms of person schemas. This is because our impressions of other people are cognitive representations (implicit personality theories) which simplify and encode the information available. Certain types of information, for example, warm and cold traits, form the heart of person schemas which we apply widely to most people we encounter for the first time. This may also be related to our self-schemas and the ideas of aschematic and schematic. Recall from what was said earlier, that schematic traits are of central importance to us whilst aschematic are not. The traits of warm and cold may be schematic because the former is positive and the latter negative. We like to see ourselves in a positive light, that is, warm for example, and hence regard this as a central or schematic trait for the impressions we form of others.

The development of a person schema for a new acquaintance may be highly influenced by what we first learn about the person (see the examples at the start of this chapter). We rapidly form a first impression and existing schemas, together with prototypes, lead us to infer a great deal about a person on the basis of limited information (Fiske, 1995). Research, as we have seen, has consistently demonstrated a **primacy effect**: information we receive first has a greater impact on the impression formed than information coming later. More recent research has shown that negative behaviour may be more influential in determining whether we like another person on first encounter than positive behaviour (Klein, 1991). The explanation for this is that we hold a prototype in our person schema that we generally like other people. Negative behaviour suggests a person is unfriendly or undesirable and therefore not nice to know.

In summary, social schemas (in the form of person and self-schemas) together with prototypes help explain why certain traits (central traits) are more influential and explain why first impressions are lasting and often slow to change.

Social schemas and self-fulfilling prophecies

A self-fulfilling prophecy is where expectations we hold about ourselves or another person cause us or the other person to behave in ways consistent with our original expectations. Basically, if you hold a self-schema making you think you are gregarious you will ensure that you are around other people a lot. In relation to another person, if you hold a person schema of your friend as humorous and possessing a good sense of humour you will behave in ways that make this come true. Thinking back to initial or first impressions, our expectations may lead us to behave in ways that elicit behaviours from others that confirm our initial expectations.

One of the most famous studies demonstrating this was conducted by Rosenthal and Jacobson (1968) called 'Pygmalion in the classroom'. Here teachers were led to expect some pupils would 'bloom' academically over the next few months whilst other pupils would not. Infant pupils had been selected at random. A year later those identified as 'bloomers' to teachers were found to be performing better than those not so identified. The same principle applies to pupils who might be labelled as 'slow to learn' (Rosenthal, 1985). Clearly how we label pupils or students in educational settings may have far-reaching consequences for how they perform and their future careers in life.

Self-fulfilling prophecies seem to be quite common (Darley and Fazio, 1980) but require a number of key steps to be present for the effect to occur. These are summarised in Figure 4.5; as you can see the whole effect is driven by the expectations held by the perceiver. Such expectations may come from person schemas, self-schemas, or in the case of stereotypes, role schemas. Role schemas may be particularly

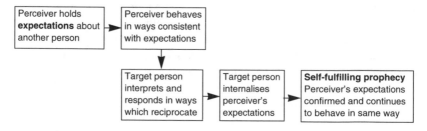

Figure 4.5 **How perceiver expectations may result in self-fulfilling prophecy**
Source: Adapted from Darley and Fazio, 1980

powerful in self-fulfilling prophecies since they engender expected behaviours and traits of people occupying influential social positions (teachers, doctors, lawyers, etc.).

Two main conditions prevent self-fulfilling prophecies: these are **compensation** and **self-verification** (Fiske and Taylor, 1991). Compensation may occur when a negative expectation is held about another person. Here the expectation that a person is unfriendly may be compensated for by the person acting in a particularly friendly way. This may change the initial expectation held. With self-verification people actively attempt to refute the label that is being applied and behave as, or say what, they are actually like. This strategy may not be very successful if the expectations are very strongly held. Generally, avoiding self-fulfilling prophecies requires your own self-schemas to be made known to another person. This will only work, however, in areas where you have self-schemas in the first place.

> Write three headings about social schemas: impression formation, stereo-types, self-fulfilling prophecies. Identify the relevant schema(s) under each heading and provide a specific example from everyday life of each.
>
> Review exercise

The cognitive miser and the heuristics of thinking

Social schemas, as we have seen, can be conceptualised into numerous general categories – person, role, self and event – with many specific schemas in each category. Some schemas will be acquired by most people in a culture, others are more idiosyncratic and reflect individual experience. Social schemas offer simplified ways of how to deal with large amounts of information in our social world. Fiske and Taylor (1991) apply the term **cognitive miser** to reflect the fact that people have a limited capacity to process social information and take shortcuts or develop simple rules to use wherever possible. Cognitive misers use strategies that make complex issues simple and produce quick answers or judgements. This has strong parallels to the idea of spontaneous and deliberative thinking that was considered in both Chapters 1 and 2. Only in special circumstances do people think more deeply – engage in deliberative thinking.

With the different types of social schemas and the vast array of specific schemas within each category, together with the principle that we are cognitive misers, you won't be surprised to learn that people employ a small number of simple rules by which to make judgements or social inferences. These rules have been called the heuristics of thinking (Tversky and Kahneman, 1974). In what follows, we will consider three of the most important heuristics – availability, anchoring and adjustment, and representativeness – and then briefly consider their relationship to social schemas.

The availability heuristic

The **availability heuristic** is a rule of thumb people use to judge the frequency of an event by the ease with which it can be brought to mind (Tversky and Kahneman, 1974). For example, imagine that you are in conversation with a friend about how frequently arguments occur between married couples. As it happens both of you are married and enjoy relationships where rows are very rare. On the basis of the social schemas you have developed both of you may significantly under-estimate the frequency of rows between married couples generally. The availability heuristic reflects your own experience of the world and may lead to erroneous or biased inferences or judgements because of this. MacLeod and Campbell (1992) show that vivid and easy-to-imagine events are often seen as more common than they actually are. Conversely, events that are dull and hard to imagine are seen as less common than they actually are. For example, because aircraft crashes are highly vivid and easy to imagine people overestimate the risk of flying (Slovic *et al.*, 1982). Gerrig and Prentice (1991) produced evidence to show that popular and best-selling fictional stories, television programmes and films create person or event schemas which may be drawn on later by the availability heuristic. Hence our judgements of frequency or commonness of events or types of personality may be based on little more than the fantasy story in a film!

The availability heuristic relies on how we both search and retrieve social information from memory. Social schemas which are easily retrieved (for example, those most commonly used and well-developed), salient because they are vivid or have strong emotional significance for the person and informed by prototypes, all contribute to explaining why the availability heuristic is widely used when making social inferences and judgements.

The representativeness heuristic

The representativeness heuristic is used to make judgements of similarity. To provide a concrete example consider the following scenario from Tversky and Kahneman (1974):

> Steve is very shy and withdrawn, invariably helpful but with little interest in people or in the world of reality. A meek and tidy soul, he has a need for order and a passion for detail.

Your task is now to decide whether Steve is an artist, librarian, former trapeze artist, driver or surgeon. Tversky and Kahneman found most participants in their study stated that Steve was a librarian. Assisting you in this social judgement task you are most likely to employ the use of prototypes – ideal schemas (see page 71). The description given of Steve above may fit many aspects of the mental representation – prototype or stereotype – that you hold of librarians.

The use of the representative heuristic would seem justified by such examples; however, people often ignore other relevant information when using this heuristic. The most important is base-rate information, which is the frequency of events in a large sample of the general population. Take the example of Steve again, and now suppose that you have been given the additional information that this description was drawn from a pool of 100 descriptions in which just 10 were of librarians, 70 were surgeons and the rest from another three categories. Would this information affect your subjective probability that Steve was in fact a librarian? Research consistently reports a base-rate fallacy – the tendency to ignore or under-use base-rate information (Nisbett and Ross, 1980; Triplet, 1992). Base-rate information is dull and hard to use, whilst a personality profile of an individual is vivid and accessible to other social schemas that we have.

The anchoring and adjustment heuristic

Tversky and Kahneman (1973) suggest that people often make judgements by starting from an initial 'anchor' and then adjusting to make the final assessment. For example, Plous (1989) asked people one of two questions: whether nuclear war had either more than a 1 in 100 chance of occurring or less than a 90 in 100 chance of occurring. Those who were given an anchor of 1 in 100 made an adjustment to arrive at 10 in 100, whilst those given an anchor of 90 in 100 adjusted downwards to 25 in 100.

Evidence that this heuristic may apply to a legal setting has been produced by Greenberg *et al.* (1986). In a simulated trial mock jurors were asked to consider verdicts that they might return against the defendant by taking either the most serious charge first or least serious first. It was found that harsher verdicts resulted from the instruction to consider the most serious charge first. In effect the instruction acted as an anchor from which the mock jurors made an adjustment.

Summary

Heuristics of thinking are mental rules of thumb that allow us to make simple judgements based on complex information. Much of the time they operate effectively and produce 'good enough' social inferences. However, they can lead to bias and error because they are shortcuts and rely more on spontaneous than on deliberative thinking. We have also seen how different social schemas and prototypes are used in our heuristic thinking. Figure 4.6 summarises the three heuristics we have considered in this section.

Review exercise

Refer to Figure 4.6 and write down two more examples of each of the three heuristics of thinking. For each example try to identify whether use of the heuristic gives an accurate judgement or whether bias/error may result.

Heuristic	Description	Example
Availability	Judgement of frequency of event by ease of bringing to mind	Estimating likelihood of an air crash as a result of ease with which can bring examples to mind
Representativeness	Used to make judgements of similarity, but people are subject to the base-rate fallacy	Extrovert description of a person linked to judgement that person is a stunt performer. But ignores number of stunt performers in the population
Anchoring and adjustment	Judgement made by starting from an initial anchor point and then adjusting to reach final position	Judging another person's ability to use the internet based on your own ability

Figure 4.6 **Three heuristics of thinking, with description and example**

Social representations

Theory and research on social representations derive from a strong sociological, European tradition and offer an analysis of human social thought at a much more collective or macro level. Social schemas, by contrast, operate at a more individual and micro level. For the past 30 years the highly influential work of Moscovici (1972) has set an agenda to make social psychology more about society and culture, rather than at an individual level and based on cognitive processes. In this section we shall first explore Moscovici's ideas about social representations and then consider their relationship to social schemas.

Understanding social representations

Moscovici (1981) defines social representations as:

> a set of concepts, statements and explanations originating in daily life in the course of inter-individual communications. They are the equivalent, in our society, of the myths and belief systems

in traditional societies; they might even be said to be the contemporary version of common sense.

(p. 181)

Four points follow from this definition: first, everyday social events are only given meaning through our interaction with other people. Second, meanings are determined by the culture or sub-culture in which we live, hence different cultures will have different rules about what is and what is not socially acceptable. Third, the more we are engaged or identify ourselves as part of a culture the better able we are to interact and communicate with other people who are part of the same culture. Fourth, the social representations approach attempts to understand everyday, common-sense aspects of our social life.

Concrete examples may help to clarify what is being said here. Moscovici claims that different cultures have different social representations for what is acceptable to eat, how to dress, how to greet people, social etiquette and appropriate non-verbal behaviour in social interaction. Many of these social behaviours create a cultural identity.

Sperber (1985) distinguishes between three levels of social representation reflecting how enduring or changeable they may be. Cultural representations are at the highest level and most enduring, difficult to change and unlikely to be influenced by any one person. Traditional representations last over a number of generations and may be influenced by major figures or leaders. Finally, fashions are representations that change rapidly within a generation. From these distinctions you might claim that Western cultures are highly influenced by fashion representations, whilst other cultures such as Chinese, Asian Indian and Moslem Arabs operate more at the level of cultural representations where change is very slow and established values are cherished and maintained.

Moscovici (1984) claims that social representations are the product of two key processes: anchoring and objectification. **Anchoring** is a process which allows new or novel information to be categorised as belonging to a particular social category we already possess. Anchoring functions to render the unfamiliar – strange, and potentially frightening – familiar and understandable. Language is of vital importance here in that it may be the first step in the categorisation process. **Objectification** is the process that turns complex and abstract ideas into specific, concrete images thus making them easier to understand. Moscovici and Hewstone (1983) identify three processes within objectification which turn complex ideas into social representations. These are summarised in Figure 4.7.

To appreciate better how social representations might work at a practical, applied level the research by Herzlich (1973) and Jodelet (1991) is of value. These researchers analysed how French people represented illness and suggested three types of representation:

1 illness as something which destroys our routines and behaviour in everyday social life;
2 illness as liberation from obligation because not at work, can adopt 'sick role' etc.; and
3 illness as an occupation or pastime, as with the hypochondriac in the extreme case.

From this it can be seen that treating illness is not only to do with medication and drugs but it also has a psychological aspect. Since social representations are mostly culture-based we would expect to discover different ones in different cultures.

Take the example of crime and think about social representations of crime in relation to anchoring and objectification. Do this for the crimes of burglary, joy riding and murder.

Progress exercise

In summary, social representations are of interest to social psychologists because: they originate from social interaction with other people; prescribe an agreed code of conduct; and offer a shared basis for understanding and communication between people (Potter and Wetherell, 1987).

Social representations and social schemas

Social representations and social schemas offer different levels of explanations of social thought and social behaviour (Augostinos and

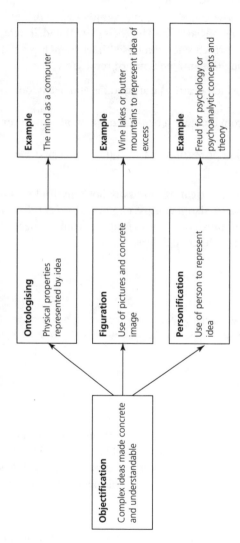

Figure 4.7 **Three processes of ontologising, figuration and personification for turning abstract ideas into common-sense understanding and social representations**
Source: **After Moscovici and Hewstone, 1983**

Walker, 1995). Social representations are at a macro level and encompass cultural beliefs, values and social traditions. By contrast social schemas operate at a micro level and focus much more on the individual and the schemas developed from experience. In a sense, they are complementary to each other since a more complete explanation and understanding of human social thought and behaviour is provided when taken together.

Both approaches suggest mental structures for how we process and organise social information. However, it is probably true to say that social schemas place greater emphasis on understanding the processes involved, whilst social representations are more interested in the content side of things.

Social schemas are more readily understandable and offer a simpler way of understanding the individual in a social context. Social representations are complex and quite abstract on first encounter. By contrast, social schemas more readily relate to cognitive psychology.

Finally, social representations offer a much better way of understanding differences and similarities between cultures than do social schemas. Social representations may better facilitate inter-cultural understanding and co-operation.

Summary

Social perception is the process through which we seek to know and understand other people; one aspect of this is impression formation. Theory and research on impression formation has centred around first impressions. Asch (1946) found some personality traits – central traits – were more influential than peripheral traits on impression formation. Implicit personality theory is a general expectation resulting from knowledge of central traits. Primacy effects are found to be more prevalent than recency effects: the latter are more likely to occur when there is a time gap between two sets of information. People manage the impression they are trying to make on other people through the techniques of self-enhancement and other-enhancement.

Social schemas are cognitive structures which represent knowledge about people and social situations. They are organised collections of knowledge stored in memory and based on past experience. Social schemas determine how information is encoded and help to process new information quickly. Four main types of schemas have been identified: person schemas, self-schemas, role schemas, and event schemas. Prototypes are special schemas representing ideal or perfect types.

A self-fulfilling prophecy is where expectations about another person cause that person to behave in ways consistent with these expectations. Self-fulfilling prophecies may be prevented through compensation and self-verification.

Conceptualising people as cognitive misers means that cognitive shortcuts such as heuristics of thinking increase in importance. Heuristics include availability, representativeness, and anchoring and adjustment. These may lead to bias or error in social inference.

Social representations are the way people cognitively represent cultural values, beliefs, and norms. Social representations are the product of the processes of anchoring and objectification. Objectification can be seen as consisting of ontologising, figuration and personification. Social representations and social schemas offer different levels of explanation, the former at a macro, cultural level and the latter at a micro, individual level. The two approaches may be complementary.

Further reading

Augostinos, M. and Walker, I. (1995) *Social Cognition: An Integrated Approach*, London: Sage Publications.
Offers whole chapters on both social schemas and social representations with critical comments on each, then attempts to compare both. Consideration is given to similarities and differences, and possibilities for integration of the two approaches.

Fiske, S. T. and Taylor, S. E. (1991) *Social Cognition*, 2nd edn, New York: McGraw-Hill.
Provides extensive coverage of social schemas in terms of what they are, what they do and how they relate to the self. Chapters are supported by extensive reference to research. Also deals quite fully with heuristics of thinking.

Moscovici, S. (1981) On social representations. In J. P. Forgas (ed.), *Social Cognition: Perspectives on Everyday Understanding*, London: Academic Press.

Well-regarded, classic article which makes Moscovici's ideas accessible and understandable. An article nearly 20 years old but sets the scene clearly about social representations.

5

Prejudice and discrimination
Origins, maintenance and reduction

A social problem

Three nail bombs exploded in different parts of London in April 1999. Whoever placed these terrible devices gave no prior warning and, because the bombs went off in a busy high street and a popular bar in Soho, many people were cruelly injured and three people died. It is hard to comprehend that an individual or small group of people could commit such anti-social and criminal acts. The perpetrators targeted ethnic groups (in Brixton people of African and Asian origin) and homosexuals (a gay bar in Soho).

In Eastern Europe in the late 1990s the Serbs adopted a policy known as 'ethnic cleansing', which was really genocide expressed differently. This resulted in over half a million Albanians, who had lived in Kosovo for generations, having to leave their homes and all their possessions, to flee to countries where they would be safe. On their way the Serbs slaughtered many men from the villages and buried them in mass graves. Extended families, a strong tradition among the Kosovan Albanians, were separated – mother from child, grandmother from granddaughter – causing despair, desolation and grief for all involved.

Social psychologists have attempted to understand the causes of prejudice, discrimination and intergroup conflict for over a hundred years. Whilst significant progress in our understanding has been made it seems that only limited success has been achieved in attempts to reduce prejudice and intergroup conflict.

In this chapter we shall consider how prejudice and intergroup conflict may arise from stereotypes (pages 95–9), intergroup relationships and group membership (pages 101–9). We will also consider the relative deprivation theory account of prejudice. Two other approaches, based on individual psychology, will also be considered – the authoritarian personality, and frustration aggression. The chapter concludes by looking at a number of strategies which may reduce prejudice, discrimination and intergroup conflict. First, we will define terms and consider some examples of prejudice and discrimination.

Prejudice may be defined as:

> an unjustified negative (or positive) attitude toward an individual based solely on that individual's membership in a group
>
> (Worchel *et al.*, 1988)

This definition is helpful since it characterises prejudice as unjustified and highlights the fact that an individual is only the target of prejudiced attitudes because he or she is perceived to be a member of a group. It is the group as a whole that the prejudicial attitudes are focused on. Note also that whilst most prejudice is concerned with negative attitudes one can be prejudiced in a positive way – for example, unjustifiably favouring an individual just because he or she is perceived to belong to a group we hold in high regard.

Discrimination refers to the actual behaviours, rather than attitudes, and may be defined as:

> Negative (or sometimes positive) actions taken towards members of a particular group because of their membership in the group.
>
> (Feldman, 1998)

Discrimination then, is the actual behaviour an individual or group of people engage in as a result of holding stereotypical and prejudiced attitudes. Whilst we normally expect discrimination to reflect and follow on from attitudes a person holds, it may often be the case that a person is prejudiced but makes no overt display of this through what they do or say. In both the examples given at the start of this chapter, extreme forms of discrimination have occurred. However, soldiers in the Serbian army may not as individuals hold prejudiced attitudes, but simply be obeying orders. Hence, discrimination can occur where an individual does not hold consistent attitudes – peer pressure and wanting to please other people as well as obeying orders may be seen in this way.

Distinguish between prejudice and discrimination by using a relevant example taken from a recent daily newspaper.

Progress exercise

Racism and sexism: old and new

Prejudiced attitudes and discriminatory behaviour can be manifest with respect to any identifiable social grouping. The most common are: racism, sexism, homophobia, ageism, intolerance of people with disabilities (both physical and mental), towards fat people, short people, tall people – you can go on adding to this list. Here we will consider racism and sexism since they are most widespread and extensively researched by social psychologists.

Racism and sexism can operate on at least two levels: first, at the individual level with prejudicial attitudes towards people of a given race or sex; and second, at an institutional level where practices maintain people of certain races or sex in subordinate roles or result in unequal service to their publics (Myers, 1996). The term 'glass ceiling' has been coined to refer to difficulties women face in reaching senior positions in organisations, although some progress has been

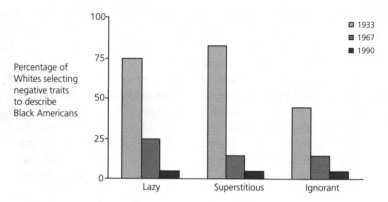

Figure 5.1 **Changes in attitudes towards Black Americans by White Americans over a 60-year period**
Source: Adapted from Dovidio and Fazio, 1992

made in the 1990s. Both racism and sexism are legislated against in Great Britain and other countries such as the United States. Research findings on North American White attitudes to Black Americans have changed over a 60-year period, as shown in Figure 5.1. Dovidio and Fazio (1992) seem to indicate that over this period tolerance between White Americans and Black Americans has improved.

However, Dovidio and Fazio (1992) point out that anti-discrimination laws mean that it is publicly unacceptable to express racist or sexist attitudes. Disappointingly, they claim that people's prejudices are still strongly held but rarely expressed openly. This has resulted in a more subtle type of racism called **new racism** (Gaertner and Dovidio, 1986; Surim *et al.*, 1995). Surim *et al.* (1995) identify three major aspects of new racism: first, denial that discriminatory practices against another group still exist. Second, irritation and antagonism towards minorities demanding equal treatment, and third, resentment that disadvantaged groups get special favourable treatment. This analysis could equally be applied to 'new sexism' as well. Racism or sexism of this sort is more covert, and may be more difficult to deal with. Social representations (see Chapter 4) are culturally determined, and it is probable that some of our deep-seated prejudices towards other social groups are determined this way also (Moscovici, 1972).

Taking the examples of homophobia, people with disabilities, and ageism identify two types of prejudice and describe two types of discriminating behaviour.

The role of stereotypes

Stereotypes may be defined as 'beliefs to the effect that all members of specific social groups share certain traits or characteristics' (Baron and Byrne, 1997). Stereotypes ignore distinguishing features of an individual by assuming that all individuals perceived to belong to a social group share the same characteristics. As such, stereotypes represent gross oversimplifications of our social world. Stereotypes may be regarded as a particular type of **role schema** (see Chapter 4) since such schemas consist of expected behaviours, traits, and beliefs, that people belonging to social groups commonly exhibit. Stereotypes are oversimplifications of our social world but useful since they help process large amounts of social information and bring order to our social life. However, their very strength is also their weakness. Campbell (1967) identified four consequences of stereotyping people:

1 Stereotypes over-estimate differences between groups;
2 Stereotypes underestimate differences between individuals within a social grouping;
3 Stereotypes distort reality since the over-estimations and under-estimations in 1 and 2 above oversimplify; and
4 Stereotypes are usually negative and serve to belittle or discriminate against groups.

Stereotypes are prevalent in our society and perpetuated by, for example, cultural norms, social norms, peer group pressure and the media.

The media (television, newspapers, the internet, films, etc.) have a powerful influence on our lives and it is reasonable to assume that how

95

groups are portrayed may serve to strengthen or reinforce existing stereotypes. For example, Archer *et al.* (1983) analysed 2000 pictures of men and women displayed in commonly read magazines and found evidence for a phenomenon they called **face-ism**. Faces of men featured much more prominently in the overall picture than faces of women. This might have the subconscious effect of men being perceived as more prominent and dominant than women – serving to perpetuate stereotypical views. Chrisler and Levy (1990) analysed the roles played by men and women in films that had won Oscars. As Figure 5.2 shows, men and women occupied stereotypical roles in these films, with women featuring highly as unemployed and males as employed in professions.

Given that Oscar-winning films are seen by tens of millions of people, we should be concerned that the film industry appears to portray men and women in stereotypical and, perhaps, sexist roles.

Men		*Women*	
Occupation	Percentage	**Occupation**	Percentage
Soldier	14	Actress	15
Sheriff	8	Prostitute	12
Criminal	8	Heiress	4
Politician	6	Teacher	4
Actor	6	Artist	4
Writer	6	Farmer's wife	4
Labourer	6	Secretary	4
Businessman	5	Businesswoman	3
Lawyer	5	Queen	3
Journalist	5	Politician	3
Boxer	4	Nurse	2
Priest	3	Maid	2
Teacher	3	Other	6
Other	17	Unemployed	34
Unemployed	4		
Total	100	Total	100

Figure 5.2 **Roles played by men and women in Oscar-winning films**
Source: Adapted from Chrisler and Levy, 1990

The features we first notice about other people tend to be their race, sex and age (Stangor *et al.*, 1992), i.e. visually salient aspects. As such we may usefully apply the two-stage model originally introduced in Chapter 1, of spontaneous and deliberative thought, to stereotyping. At the spontaneous stage we may automatically notice salient features about another person such as age, sex, race, dress and make a spontaneous categorisation to a pre-existing stereotype. Having done this initial categorisation certain emotions, assumptions and behaviours may follow. This may result in prejudice and discrimination if the stereotype is a negative one and relates to a social group we do not like.

The stereotype rebound effect

Encouraging deliberative thought should result in helping to prevent a person becoming automatically stereotyped since deliberative thought requires obtaining more information, and questioning the categorisation or stereotyping initially made. This may cause a stereotype to be suppressed. Macrae *et al.* (1994) reported disturbing evidence for a stereotype rebound effect. In this study participants were given a photograph of a male skinhead and then required to write a 'day in the life' of a typical skinhead. Half the participants were warned before writing the 'day in the life' not to use stereotypic preconceptions. The other half of the participants were given no such warning. Participants were given five minutes to complete this task and were then provided with a picture of another skinhead and asked to describe him but without any prior instructions. The contents of the descriptions were analysed and rated on a stereotypic scale. From Figure 5.3 it can be seen that participants asked not to use stereotypic preconceptions in their first description showed a 'rebound' effect in their second description, that is the stereotype appeared more strongly the second time. The general point to be drawn from this study is that suppression of a stereotype may result in its being more strongly expressed on a subsequent occasion.

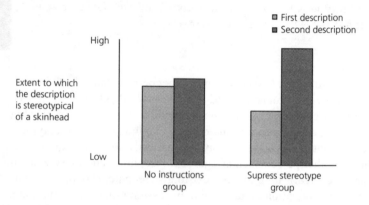

Figure 5.3 **The rebound effect of suppressing stereotype on the first description of a picture of a skinhead, but not on the second description**
Source: **Adapted from Macrae *et al.*, 1994**

Stereotypes and expectations

Stereotypes may guide people to seek out information that is consistent with the stereotype, with ambiguous behaviour on the part of another person often being interpreted as stereotype-consistent (Darley and Gross, 1983). Stereotype-generated expectations may, therefore, lead us to see what we expect, or even want, to see. Stereotypes may also lead us to behave in ways that will confirm our expectations leading to a self-fulfilling prophecy. In a work context, for example, Binning *et al.* (1988) showed that interviewers who held prior expectations that a candidate was not appropriate for the job looked for negative information when asking questions. Conversely, where interviewers held prior expectations that a candidate was highly suitable they looked for positive information.

Stereotypes, then, are powerful cognitive structures, akin to role schemas, that organise, simplify and structure our social world. They ignore individual differences when assigning an individual to a stereotypical group and lead to prejudice and discrimination.

Think of a distinctive social group that is part of the teenage sub-culture, such as hippies, punks or goths. Write down the stereotypic aspects that you think apply to the whole group. Then think of an individual whom you know who is a member (in the loose sense) of such a teenage sub-culture. Describe this person. Now compare your stereotype of the group with your description of the individual. Identify similarities and differences. What differences do you notice between the stereotype and the description of the person you know?

Realistic group conflict

Stereotypes operate at an individual level but serve to categorise oneself and other people into different social groups. However, how groups interact plays an important role, and one approach to investigating this has been through **realistic conflict theory** (Sherif, 1966). The basic idea here is that prejudice and discrimination 'derive from direct competition between two or more groups for scarce or valued resources' (Baron and Byrne, 1997). Sherif argued that groups that shared goals which were mutually exclusive (i.e. one achieves a goal at the expense of the other) will exhibit competition. On the other hand, groups that have the same goals which require both groups to work together to achieve will co-operate. We will look at the former here and the latter later in this chapter (see pages 118–24).

Sherif's 'Robber's Cave' experiment

Realistic group conflict was explored in one of the most famous field experiments ever conducted in social psychology, by Sherif (1966), called the 'Robber's Cave' study. Sherif and his researchers devised a special summer camp for 11–12-year-old boys which took place over a three-week period. During the first week the boys were divided into two groups and assigned living quarters that were a few hundred yards apart. The boys named their own groups – Rattlers and Eagles – and developed strong friendships with other boys within their group. The boys engaged in behaviour which enhanced the identity and value of the group they had been assigned to, for example, playing team games and making flags and t-shirts with symbols representing the group.

During this first stage no competitive activities took place between the Rattlers and the Eagles.

Following this, in the second week, Sherif and his colleagues staged a number of activities that brought the two groups into competition. The winning group would receive prizes and a trophy. During the week of competition, prejudice and hostility developed between the two groups, starting with name-calling but soon developing into more hostile acts such as the Eagles' burning of the Rattlers' flag. This resulted in counteractions by the Rattlers in which they raided the living quarters of the Eagles, generally wreaked havoc and stole personal possessions. At the end of the second week Sherif (1966) summarised the relationship between the two groups:

> If an outsider had entered the situation at this point with no information about preceding events, he could only have concluded on the basis of their behaviour that these boys were wicked, disturbed, and vicious bunches of youngsters.

> (p. 85)

Fortunately, as we shall see on pages 118–19, matters were resolved between the two groups when they were required to work co-operatively.

Evaluation

Similar consequences of realistic group conflict have been found amongst different cultures (Diab, 1970). Diab conducted a similar study in the Lebanon using ten Christian and eight Moslem 11-year-old boys. Two random groups were established, being of mixed religions, one named the 'Friends' and the other 'Red Genie'. The latter group were aggressive and competitive, and the former more co-operative. The 'Red Genie' group not only stole from the 'Friends' group but also from amongst themselves. The study ended before the final, co-operative stage because the 'Red Genie' group were so aggressive and disruptive. However, attempts at replication among scout groups in this country have not shown dramatic effects (Tyerman and Spencer, 1983). It may be that the North American culture is particularly competitive and fosters such conflict. It may also be that the complexity of Sherif's original study is too difficult to replicate, and hence it may have to be regarded as a unique field study. This questions the extent to which the findings can be generalised. An important criticism of Sherif's study, and those like it, is that two important variables are confounded – group membership and competition between groups. It may be that group membership on its own is sufficient for intergroup bias and conflict to emerge. It is to this that we now turn.

Group membership

Tajfel (1978) presented and developed a highly influential approach in British social psychology which considered the importance of group membership for prejudice and intergroup conflict. This was empirically investigated using what has become known as the **minimum group paradigm**. These findings were integrated into social identity theory, which was refined and developed by Turner (1985) to be named social categorisation theory. We shall consider each in turn.

The minimal group paradigm

Tajfel (1970) developed a research technique to investigate intergroup discrimination where group membership *without* competition or even interaction between groups took place. Tajfel showed that even when the basis for an individual to be categorised as belonging to a group was trivial or unimportant members discriminated against the **outgroup** (the other group) in favour of the **ingroup** (the group the individual was a member of). The minimal group paradigm involves providing participants, originally British schoolboys were used, with a matrix similar to that shown in Figure 5.4. Participants were told that the numbers represent points or money that could be allocated to an ingroup and an outgroup member.

Tajfel assigned schoolboys to one of two groups on a random basis. However, the schoolboys were led to believe the assignment to a group had been on the basis of their expressed preferences for the artwork of one of two artists: Klee or Kandinsky. The schoolboys did not know who else was in their group or who in the other group, and were given no opportunity for interaction with other group members. Generally, it was found that points were allocated in such a way as to favour their own group (i.e. the ingroup).

Ingroup member	7	8	9	10	11	12	13	14	15	16	17	18	19
Outgroup member	1	3	5	7	9	11	13	15	17	19	21	23	25
Strategy	(c)		◀— (d) —▶				(a)						(b)

Figure 5.4 Minimum group paradigm matrix used by Tajfel (1970)
Note: Selecting column (a) represents a fairness strategy, (b) maximising joint profit, (c) maximum difference, and (d) ingroup favouritism.

If you consider the matrix shown in Figure 5.4 a number of different strategies for distributing points or money between the two groups are represented. These are:

(a) Fairness – the equal distribution of points between the two groups, represented by the 13:13 column.
(b) Maximum joint profit – maximising points for both groups regardless of which group gets most. Represented by column 19:25.
(c) Maximum difference – maximising the greatest difference of points between groups. Represented by column 7:1.
(d) Ingroup favouritism – allocating more points to the ingroup than the outgroup. Represented by columns to the left of 13:13.

The ingroup bias in the allocation of points by the schoolboys in Tajfel's (1970) original experiments has proved to be a robust phenomenon, occurring across different types of groups and in factory settings for wage bargaining (Brown, 1978).

Tajfel and Billig (1974), in an attempt to eradicate the effect, went as far as to toss a coin in front of participants to allocate them to a group. Even when allocated on an explicitly random basis, participants still demonstrated ingroup bias when allocating points.

Evaluation

Criticisms of the minimal group paradigm technique have been to do with the highly artificial nature of the task, and that the paradigm creates demand characteristics in participants to which they conform (Gerard and Hoyt, 1974). The task may be regarded as highly artificial since rarely do we have to allocate resources (points or money) to an ingroup or outgroup on the basis of set, constrained alternatives as shown in the matrix in Figure 5.4. Given this, it may be difficult to generalise the results to real-life situations. A second way in which the task may be regarded as artificial is that when groups are required to take away points from an ingroup and outgroup, instead of award points, the ingroup bias or favouritism effect is weak and sometimes not present (Hewstone *et al.*, 1981). With respect to the demand characteristics criticism, the claim here is that participants, having virtually no information other than group membership, act according to social norms of competitiveness between groups. Participants may also conform to what they believe are the expectations of the experimenter – that they will favour their own group at the expense of the outgroup. However, how valid this is as a criticism is open to question, since other empirical research reports that it is extremely difficult to get participants to follow a co-operative pattern of points allocation on the matrix (Hogg *et al.*, 1986). Nevertheless the findings of ingroup favouritism have been generally accepted as evidence of the consequence of group membership.

Draw up a matrix, similar to that shown in Figure 5.4, but this time where points or money are being *deducted* from an ingroup or outgroup. Identify: ingroup favouritism, fairness and maximum joint profit on your matrix.

Progress exercise

Social identity theory

Social identity theory (Tajfel and Turner, 1986) states that being a member of a particular social group results in individuals gaining their sense of identity from that social group. The theory further states that individuals make an evaluation primarily by making comparisons between a group they are a member of and other outgroups. Social identity is different to personal identity, since the latter derives from personality characteristics and personal relationships with other individuals (Turner, 1982). Social identity then 'consists of those aspects of an individual's self-image that derive from social categories to which he perceives himself belonging' (Tajfel and Turner, 1986, p. 16). One further factor required to make social identity theory work is the need that people have to maintain a high level of self-esteem or self-regard (see Chapter 1). Accepting or perceiving yourself to be a member of a particular group is not enough: to maintain self-esteem the group membership must be seen as positive and self-enhancing. If the society in which you live values a social group that you are a member of then this will follow through to have a positive effect on your own self-esteem. If society does not value or denigrates a social group you are a member of then your self-esteem will be affected in a negative way (Brown, 1995).

One way to investigate these claims is through situations which pose a threat to a person's social identity. Social identity theory would predict that to maintain a positive social identity in the face of a threat should result in individuals increasing their perceived differences between groups so as to bolster the identity of the social group they belong to. Breakwell (1978) conducted a study with teenage boys who were keen football supporters. Breakwell classified some of the teenagers as 'genuine' fans because they attended all the home matches of their team, and others as 'long range' fans since they rarely went to see their team play live. Breakwell claimed that the 'long range' group should have their identity threatened since they were not categorised as real fans. When individuals from both groups were asked about the importance of certain characteristics of fans such as loyalty and knowledge, the threatened group gave them greater emphasis than the unthreatened group. This is shown in Figure 5.5.

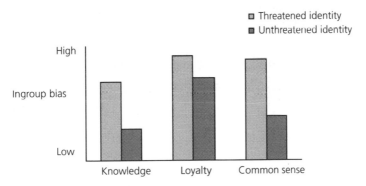

Figure 5.5 Degree of ingroup bias shown by football fans classified as 'real' or 'long range'. The latter group has its identity threatened by this classification
Source: Adapted from Breakwell, 1978

Earlier we considered the effect on the individual of being a member of a highly or a poorly valued social group. Privileged groups such as people who work, people who are physically and mentally healthy, etc., maintain their status and self-esteem by sharing ingroup favouritism (Brown, 1995). But what of people who belong to low status groups? Being a member of such a group should bring with it negative social identity – so what do individuals do? One strategy is to distance themselves from the social group, another is to emphasise the aspects of the social group that are positive. But neither strategy changes the low status in which the social group is held. A more radical strategy would be for the group members to lobby and campaign for social and economic changes in an attempt to alter the status in which the group is held. Ellemers *et al.* (1993) provided empirical support to two key factors which need to be present for this to happen. These are that status differences between the two groups should be unstable, and the status differences must be seen as unfair. History can attest to numerous examples of oppressed groups challenging authority and the status quo, resulting in a re-evaluation of the social standing of the groups.

Social identity theory offers a good explanation of why members of an ingroup favour themselves over and above an outgroup. Ingroup bias may form the basis of prejudice and discrimination leading to intergroup conflict. Real conflict is not necessarily required, however: it may be that individuals perceive competition between in- and outgroups even when it is not present.

Self-categorisation theory

Social identity theory can only work if a person categorises him- or herself as belonging to a particular social grouping: you can hardly show ingroup bias if you do not regard yourself as a member of that particular ingroup! Turner (1985) recognised this critical feature and developed **self-categorisation theory** to explain social identity. In order to categorise yourself as belonging or not belonging to a social group, Turner *et al.* (1987) claim that you hold cognitive representations of the typical or ideal/aspects of the social group. These are called **prototypes**, which we considered in relation to person schemas in Chapter 4. For example, we might hold a prototype for a hippy which might include, for the man, wearing long hair and a beard, clothes embroidered with flowers, saying everything is 'cool' and 'yeah man'. Individuals are more or less prototypical of a social group and the more an individual resembles the prototype for a social group, the more the person is prototypical of the group (Hogg and Hardie,

1991). Prototypes also have the consequence of minimising differences within a group and maximising differences between groups. Think about a prototype for a punk, and contrast it with your prototype for a hippy. To influence behaviour of ingroup members the prototype for a social group needs to be shared or strongly agreed upon by the group members.

Get a friend to do this exercise with you. First, separately list all the social groups that you think both you and your friend are members of. Second, identify those you agree with for yourself and those you disagree with. Finally, determine whether or not you are a member of the groups on the 'disagree' list.

Progress exercise

Since social identity is based on self-categorisation it is important to understand the ease with which social categories are accessible or brought to mind. A number of factors have been identified; these include the ones listed here.

* The extent to which group members use the word 'we' to refer to the group. The word 'we' has positive associations in contrast to using 'they' to refer to a group (Dovidio and Gaertner, 1993).
* Direct reminders of being a member of a group (for example, by the use of titles or labels).
* The presence of outgroup members (imagine being in the common room as a psychology student talking to five students studying chemistry!).
* Being in a minority as a social group; and where conflict and rivalry exist between groups (Smith and Mackie, 1995).

Outgroup homogeneity

One interesting consequence of self-categorisation is what is called the **outgroup homogeneity effect**. This is the tendency to perceive outgroup members as more similar or homogeneous than ingroup members (Abrams and Hogg, 1998). This is captured in everyday language by such phrases as 'they're all alike' and 'they all think the same way'. It becomes self-perpetuating since such a view then justifies generalising from the behaviour of one person to the whole group. Platz and Hosch (1988) conducted a study using counter clerks in Texas convenience shops. Three confederates of the experiment – an Anglo-American, an African-American and a Mexican-American – each went into a number of different shops and were served by counter clerks who were either Anglo-American, African-American or Mexican-American. As shown in Figure 5.6 the counter clerks were best able to identify customers from their own group, thus demonstrating that there is a common and prevailing tendency to see members of other groups (outgroups) as looking alike or less distinguishable from each other.

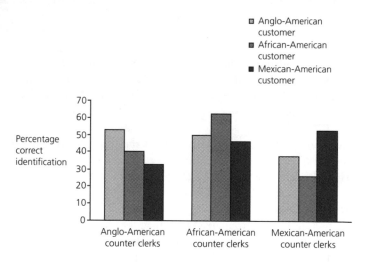

Figure 5.6 **Identification of different customer types by three groups of counter clerks**
Source: **Adapted from Platz and Hosch, 1988**

Notice that this is a field study so does have the strength of using a real-life situation. However, we do not know, for example, how often the counter clerks in their day-to-day work served each of these three groups and how much exposure to each of these three groups they had outside of work.

One exception to the outgroup homogeneity effect is when the ingroup represents a minority group. Here the minority group is seen to be more homogeneous or the same by both ingroup members and outgroups (Brown and Smith, 1989).

In the preceding sections quite a detailed look at how group membership influences attitudes and behaviour has been provided. Numerous criticisms of the approach have been made. For example, the minimal group paradigm is irrelevant to everyday life since we do not go around allocating points to ingroup and outgroup members (Schiffman and Wicklund, 1992). Criticisms have been made of social identity theory: that it does not represent a proper theory since there is no attempt to understand what individuals bring to a group. This concerns whether or not the person is able to choose to be a member of a group; for example, if you are Chinese you have no choice about being seen as a member of the Chinese ethnic group. However, being a member of a football club is something you have choice over. Additionally, individuals may be held in high or low esteem by the group as a whole and are rarely group members on an equitable basis. Despite all this the approach has been highly influential and is regarded as an extremely valuable way of explaining and understanding prejudice, discrimination and intergroup conflict.

Relative deprivation theory

It would seem intuitively correct for any explanation of prejudice and discrimination to include consideration of economic factors. Economic in this context may be to do with the general health or otherwise of a country's economy as well as the standard of living an individual or identified social grouping enjoys. As far back as 1940, Hovland and Sears noticed that the economic recession in America during the 1930s was associated with an increase in anti-Black violence and lynchings perpetrated by White people. Hovland and Sears (1940) attempted to explain this on the basis of frustration and aggression (see pages 117–18) resulting in scapegoating of a vulnerable minority group. Due to inconsistent findings this explanation was replaced by what has become known as **relative deprivation theory**.

Relative deprivation theory (Gurr, 1970; Walker and Pettigrew, 1984) recognises that absolute levels of personal hardship are less important in explaining prejudice and discrimination than relative deprivation. The focus here is the discrepancy that may exist between the standard of living a person or group of people currently have and the *expectations* of a standard of living the individual or group believe he/she or they should have. Relative deprivation theory states that the larger the gap between reality and expectations, the greater the social discontent felt, which results in prejudice and intergroup conflict. People's expectations are largely determined by two factors: comparisons an individual makes with his or her recent past, and comparisons with other groups (Runciman, 1966). Comparisons with other groups require that there is perceived similarity between one's own group (ingroup) and the other group (outgroup). Comparison between an ingroup and outgroup may result in feelings of deprivation or gratification; the latter is where you perceive your own group to be better off than the other, outgroup. Figure 5.7 summarises the key elements of relative deprivation theory.

Vanneman and Pettigrew (1972) conducted a classic study which demonstrated the relationship between relative deprivation and prejudice. One thousand White voters in America were questioned concerning their perceptions about:

1 whether they thought they were doing better or worse than other White voters like themselves; and
2 whether they thought they were doing better or worse compared to Black Americans.

Vanneman and Pettigrew called 1 'egoistic' deprivation when Whites felt they were doing worse than other White voters; and 2 'fraternalist' deprivation when Whites felt they were doing worse than Blacks. Gratification in each of these comparisons is where the White voter felt he or she was doing better than other White voters or Blacks as a group. Prejudice was measured by attitudes to individuals (either White or Black) or toward events such as race riots, segregation and government measures to alleviate poverty. As Figure 5.8 shows, the highest levels of prejudice were shown by White voters who felt both egoistically and fraternalistically deprived. Figure 5.8 also shows that fraternalistic deprivation resulted in higher levels of prejudice for both types of measures than egoistic deprivation.

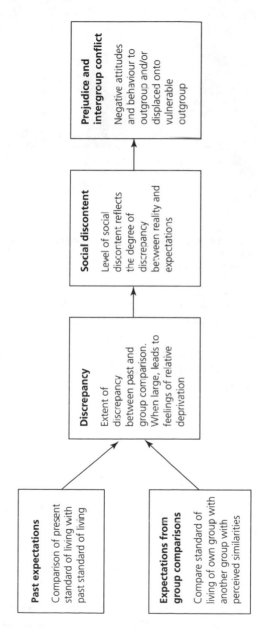

Past expectations

Comparison of present standard of living with past standard of living

Expectations from group comparisons

Compare standard of living of own group with another group with perceived similarities

Discrepancy

Extent of discrepancy between past and group comparison. When large, leads to feelings of relative deprivation

Social discontent

Level of social discontent reflects the degree of discrepancy between reality and expectations

Prejudice and intergroup conflict

Negative attitudes and behaviour to outgroup and/or displaced onto vulnerable outgroup

Figure 5.7 **Key elements and stages in the relative deprivation theory of prejudice and intergroup conflict**

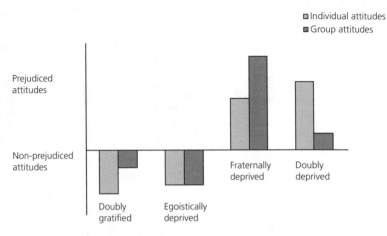

Figure 5.8 **Prejudiced and non-prejudiced attitudes resulting from individual and group comparisons**
Source: **Adapted from Vanneman and Pettigrew, 1972**

One shortcoming of this study is that whilst attitudes were measured this does not necessarily produce evidence that people will actually behave in a discriminatory or negative way to those who are better off than oneself when feeling deprived. Nevertheless, subsequent research has generally supported these findings (Bobo, 1988), and that this occurs with other ethnic comparisons, such as Muslim and Indian Hindus (Tripathi and Srivastava, 1981).

Factors which may moderate or reduce the effects of relative deprivation include permeability of group boundaries – this is where it is possible to become a member of a well-off group. Social mobility may also offset the effects of deprivation by allowing an individual to move from one social group to another (Wright *et al.*, 1990). In more extreme forms, social unrest (riots or demonstrations) may effect change of treatment of a social group through changes in government policy, allocation of more resources, etc. (Klandermans, 1984).

Evaluation

Relative deprivation theory provides important insights into the psychological consequences of economic hardship, but proposes that living standards and personal satisfaction are relative rather than

Progress exercise

List the key aspects of your own standard of living in relation to house, access to car, amount of spending money, use of computer, etc. Take away the five most important items on this list that would make you feel deprived. Get a friend to do the same exercise and compare the 'deprivation factors'. Explain any differences.

absolute. The approach emphasises group comparisons and hence has similarities with social identity theory. Both theories rely on people's cognitions and perceptions of injustice. However, with social identity theory, the identification of an individual with a group is of central importance. With relative deprivation theory such social identification is taken for granted and it is the results of social comparisons that are of central concern. Neither of these two theories has much to say about how we go about deciding or choosing which groups to compare our own with.

Individual approaches

The emphasis of this chapter has been on cognitive social psycho-logical approaches to prejudice and discrimination. Given the importance of the topic area you will not be surprised to learn that there are many other approaches as well. Here we will look at two that focus on the individual in relation to personality and emotions.

The authoritarian personality

By far the most influential and important approach attempting to relate a personality type to prejudice was that suggested by Adorno *et al.* (1950). Adorno and his colleagues were interested to under-stand and explain how people in Nazi Germany during the Second World War submitted to the demands of authority and committed appalling acts of inhumanity resulting in the Holocaust. Drawing on Freudian psychoanalytic concepts, Adorno *et al.* (1950) suggested that prejudicial attitudes are associated with a particular personality type that they called the **authoritarian personality**. The authoritarian personality is characterised by somebody who is submissive to the authority of somebody *higher* in status and power than themselves. At the same time, this type of person is authoritarian with people *lower* in status and power than themselves.

Adorno and his colleagues thought that this personality type came about as a result of early childhood experiences where parents were harsh and punishing. Such a parental style was also supposed to strongly discourage or forbid unconventional behaviour and bring up the child to adhere strongly to social and cultural conventions prevailing at the time. For the child this results in feelings of anger and aggression, as well as an inability to express sexual impulses. Since, according to Adorno, the parents were fearful and punishing figures for the child, these feelings could not be expressed by the child towards the parents. As a result, anger and aggression is projected outwards (a Freudian defence mechanism) onto outgroups or other groups of people who are vulnerable or in weak positions in a society. In a sense, the authoritarian personality uses weak and/or vulnerable groups as **scapegoats** for their own aggressive feelings. Additionally, the authoritarian personality requires such scapegoats to act in puritanical ways because as a child (and presumably later as an adult) he or she was unable to express sexual feelings.

To measure the authoritarian personality, Adorno initially developed a questionnaire to measure anti-Semitism, based on the original concern surrounding Nazi Germany. However, because the researchers had established a link between ethnocentrism (anti-Semitism being an example) and right-wing political views, the **F-scale** was developed. This represented an anti-democratic or authoritarian type of person where the 'F' stood for *Fascism*. The F-scale is made up of nine components, including conventionalism, authoritarian submission, authoritarian aggression, superstition, preoccupation with power, and puritanical sexual attitudes. Each component has four or five questions, giving a questionnaire with just under 50 items in total. Figure 5.9 gives three items on the questionnaire representing three different components.

Literally thousands of studies have been conducted using the F-scale to investigate aspects of prejudice, ethnocentrism and various forms of discrimination (Christie and Cook, 1958). Research on the F-scale produced evidence for authoritarian personalities being likely to obey authoritarian figures, be dogmatic, give out harsher sentences

Component of F-scale	Example of question from F-scale
Conventionalism	Obedience and respect for authority are the most important virtues children should learn
Superstition	Some day it will probably be shown that astrology can explain a lot of things
Puritanical sexual attitudes	Homosexuality is a particularly rotten form of delinquency and ought to be severely punished

Figure 5.9 **Examples of questions from the F-scale**
Source: **From Sanford, 1956**

as a mock jury member in simulated courtroom trials, and place trust in authority.

Evaluation of the F-scale

Whilst the F-scale attracted a huge amount of research there are both methodological and conceptual shortcomings that led to its becoming outdated. Methodologically the problem is that all the items on the F-scale are worded in the same way (where agreement scored as evidence of authoritarianism). This means that a high score – authoritarian personality – may result more from a person's tendency to agree with statements than the underlying personality type. This is known as an **acquiescent response set**. Consequently we cannot know if a high score indicates authoritarianism or a person's tendency to agree, or a mixture of both. In short, the F-scale is not valid.

On a conceptual level, correlations consistently reflected a relationship between level of education and authoritarianism: the higher the level of educational attainment the lower the score on the F-scale (Christie, 1954). This means that authoritarianism may reflect more how an individual is socialised in a certain social class than the Freudian explanations subscribed to by Adorno. A further conceptual problem is that the F-scale only deals with extreme, right-wing political attitudes and it is recognised that prejudicial attitudes may come from left- and right-wing extremists. This latter point was taken up by Rokeach (1960) who suggested that people who subscribe to extreme left- or right-wing political views have closed minds and exhibit dogmatism.

The authoritarian personality now

Renewed interest in the authoritarian personality came as a result of Altmeyer's (1981) production of a reliable and valid scale which attempts to address the above criticisms. Altmeyer (1998) produced a Right Wing Authoritarian Scale based on a much narrower conception of authoritarianism. The R.W.A. scale is based on just three components – authoritarian submission, authoritarian aggression, and conventionalism. Figure 5.10 provides an example of each of these components.

Component of Right Wing Authoritarian scale	Example of question from R.W.A. scale
Authoritarian submission	It is always better to trust the judgement of the proper authorities in Government and religion than to listen to the noisy rabble-rousers in our society
Authoritarian aggression	It would be best for everyone if the proper authorities censored magazines so that people could not get their hands on trashy and disgusting material
Conventionalism	There is no 'one right way' to live life; everybody has to create their own way

Figure 5.10 **Examples of questions from each of the three components of the Right Wing Authoritarian scale**
Source: **Adapted from Altmeyer, 1998**
Note: **The conventionalism question is worded such that disagreement scores towards right wing authoritarianism.**

Research based on the R.W.A. scale has reported people who scored high on authoritarianism as being prejudiced towards a number of groups including homosexuals and people with AIDS. Research has also shown such individuals supporting religious fundamentalism, traditional gender roles and being punitive towards criminals (Altmeyer, 1996).

It is now widely accepted that authoritarianism is a result of early socialisation by family, peer groups and culture rather than the Freudian explanations used by Adorno. It is interesting to see such a strong belief amongst some social psychologists that a person's underlying traits and personality offer the best explanation for the widespread occurrence of prejudice and discrimination that exists in not only our society, but nearly all, if not all, societies in the world. It could be that this focus on the individual may, in part, be explained by the fundamental attribution error that we encountered in Chapter 3.

Allocate each of the following items from the R.W.A. scale to one of the three components mentioned above.

a   This country would work a lot better if certain groups of troublemakers would just shut up and accept their group's traditional place in society.
b   A woman's place should be wherever she wants to be. The days when women were submissive to their husbands and social conventions belong strictly to the past.
c   What our country needs most is discipline, with everyone following our leaders in unity.

Progress exercise

Frustration and aggression

Dollard *et al.* (1939) proposed that aggressive behaviour always presupposes the emotional state of frustration, and that frustration usually results in aggressive acts. In this context discrimination and intergroup conflict are aggressive acts. However, we do not behave aggressively towards everybody but our aggression is generally aimed at those who are least able to retaliate. This explains scapegoating since social groups that become scapegoats are both disliked and made to blame for actions for which they are not responsible. Scapegoating may be more prevalent when people are threatened themselves, such as when somebody loses their job during economic depression, or when someone has very low self-esteem.

However, whilst the simplicity of the theory is attractive, it has certain shortcomings. For example, it does not explain why some people have low tolerances for frustration and others high tolerances. More importantly it has been accepted that frustration is neither necessary nor sufficient for producing aggressive acts in people (Berkowitz, 1962).

Reducing prejudice and discrimination

The different approaches to prejudice and discrimination that we have considered have implications for how we might go about changing attitudes and behaviour. Three that have received extensive consideration and good support are: setting superordinate goals; the contact hypothesis; and recategorisation. We shall consider each in turn. On a more general level, educational attainment and specific educational programmes aimed at understanding disadvantaged or discriminated against groups have been shown to have positive effects (Langer *et al.*, 1985).

Setting superordinate goals

Cast your mind back to Sherif's field experiments described on pages 99–101, where conflict between the Eagles and the Rattlers had escalated. In the third and last week of the summer camp Sherif set both groups superordinate tasks – goals which could only be achieved by both groups co-operating and working together. Sherif caused the water supply to fail and the camp lorry to break down; these events were set up in such a way that only the combined efforts of the two groups could sort the problems out.

Sherif found that superordinate tasks did reduce intergroup hostility but only when there were a number of different tasks for the boys to co-operate over. After working on just one task the groups reverted to intergroup hostilities. However, after a week working co-operatively on numerous tasks, hostilities were reduced and cross-group friendships developed. Sherif observed that for superordinate goals to reduce hostility both groups have to:

- value the task; and
- there must be equal contributions from both groups.

Evaluation

Subsequent research has shown that superordinate goals do not reduce intergroup hostility if they fail to achieve the goal (Worchel *et al.*,

1977). Also, if groups participate in superordinate goals over a long period of time the danger of groups merging to be seen as one is resisted. This results in groups acting to re-establish and assert their identities, with possible intergroup conflict re-emerging (Gaertner *et al.*, 1989). Superordinate goals work where there is success and over a short period of time. As such they do not offer a longer term solution to prejudice and discrimination.

The contact hypothesis

As far back as 1954 Gordon Allport, a highly influential social psychologist, suggested that contact between majority and minority groups should reduce prejudice and discrimination. The underlying idea is that contact and interaction between people who are prejudiced and those they are prejudiced against will dispel stereotypes, make individuals appear more individual and create more positive attitudes between groups. Mere contact appears insufficient and Gaertner *et al.* (1990) have identified three conditions most likely to foster positive attitudes towards outgroups.

1 Contact should take place between groups that have relatively similar status.
2 Contact must involve interaction and bring people close personally; just being physically in contact is not enough.
3 Contact should involve working together co-operatively to achieve similar goals.

A classic experiment demonstrating the effects of different status levels was conducted by Blanchard *et al.* (1975). Here White American airmen engaged in management training with a White and a Black person, both of whom were confederates of the experimenter. One third were told the confederates were more competent than the airmen, one third the same and one third of lower competence. After training the airmen were told they had done either well or poorly. The researchers measured the White airmen's perceived competence of the Black co-trainee.

As can be seen from Figure 5.11, White airmen liked the Black confederate more when the team were successful, and overall, more as the competence of the Black co-worker increased.

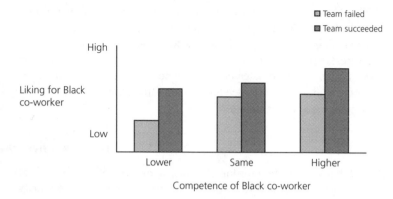

Figure 5.11 **Status and team success on liking for a Black co-worker**
Source: **Adapted from Blanchard *et al.*, 1975**

One of the most important and influential education techniques for fostering contact between schoolchildren in mixed ethnic classes in school is the **jigsaw method** (Aronson *et al.*, 1978; Aronson, 1999). To understand how this works consider the example given in Figure 5.12. Here 25 pupils in a class are learning about and discussing domestic pets; the class is put into five groups of five pupils. It is important that each group has an ethnic mix reflecting the ethnic mix of the class as well as possible. The teacher allocates a pet to each child in the group and provides information about the pet to the child. The key point here is that the group of five children as a whole can only learn about pets by pooling information and working co-operatively. Before this, however, all of the children allocated the same pet across the five groups meet to discuss their pet and decide how best to present the information to the others in their mixed pet group.

The pioneering work done on the jigsaw method by Aronson *et al.* (1978) and Aronson (1999) has shown that not only does this technique promote effective learning but that much higher levels of interpersonal interaction are sustained amongst the schoolchildren, that individual self-esteem is enhanced and that greater understanding across different racial and ethnic groups is achieved. The jigsaw method, which is sometimes referred to as **co-operative learning groups**, has the four key characteristics listed below:

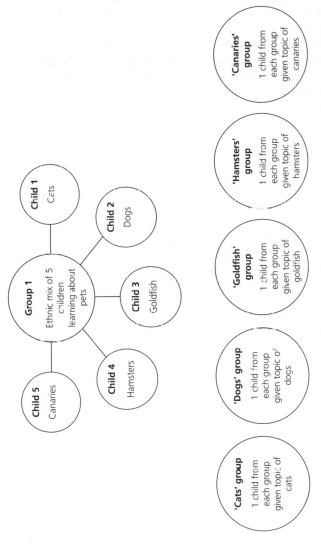

Figure 5.12 Jigsaw technique of co-operative learning exemplified using a class of twenty-five ethnically mixed children

Notes:
(a) Five groups are formed, with each child being given a different pet topic.
(b) Five same pet groups also interact.

1   Most importantly, learning is achieved through co-operation rather than competition between pupils, and children working in small groups are interdependent on each other for their learning.

2   Interaction between children is high and that between the teacher and children low compared to normal classroom learning experiences.

3   Equal status between children in mixed ethnic groups is achieved because each child has information of the same importance as the other children.

4   The schoolchildren see that the process/method is overseen by the teacher thus investing it with institutional support.

Evaluation

Slavin (1983) reviewed 14 published studies using variations of the jigsaw method and found that 11 showed educational and social improvement and three no difference. Miller and Davidson-Podgorny (1987) reviewed another 11 studies and found all of them to report significant advantages. Generally then, the jigsaw method has consistent, positive effects on reducing prejudice and discrimination, and fostering interethnic and interracial understanding. However, a lot of planning and continual management on the part of the teacher and school is required for the method to operate properly. In studies where each child or student in the group does not have equal status, for example, where mixed ethnic groups are just put together and taught in more traditional ways, no beneficial effects have been seen (Cohen, 1984).

Many governments in different countries have introduced de-segregation education policies in an attempt to reduce prejudice in children. For example, busing policies in the United States to produce schools with a mix of cultures, and Black and White children; or attempts to have mixed Catholic and Protestant schools in Northern Ireland. However, only when contact meets the above three criteria is a degree of success achieved. Slavin (1983) demonstrated that co-operative learning between individuals from different groups is important. Hewstone and Brown (1986) suggested that attitude change comes about when groups interact and when individuals are seen as typical of their particular groups.

Recategorisation

Given the importance of self-categorisation in creating an individual's social identity, strategies that attempt to get people to recategorise themselves may also be a way of reducing prejudice. Two types of recategorisation are possible: first, two different groups might merge to form one larger group; and second, one social group might be divided into two or more sub-groups.

With respect to merging groups, people of different cultures are generally resistant to losing their cultural identity in favour of another culture (Jones, 1986). One strategy might be to select out the best features of each of the groups and create a new group with these features. However, agreeing on the best features and then getting individuals to agree to adopt a new social identity is a very hard task indeed. In general, the approach of merging groups to create a single social identity, whilst a good idea in principle, proves to be extremely difficult to operationalise and implement.

The other strategy, of sub-dividing social groups into smaller groups, if followed to a logical conclusion would result in each person seeing themselves as unique with social identities deriving from group membership being less meaningful than personal identity. An experiment by Gaertner et al. (1989) investigated the effects of both recategorisation strategies. Here students were first divided into three person groups to work on a task, after which traditional ingroup/ outgroup attitudes were detected. The researchers then asked two groups either to think of themselves as one large group of six, or six 'groups' of one. Both recategorisations reduced ingroup bias; those asked to think of themselves as unique individuals subsequently thought less highly of the other two group members. By contrast, those asked to think of themselves as a group of six thought more highly of members of the outgroup.

For each of the three methods used by social psychologists in attempts to reduce prejudice – setting superordinate goals, contact and recategorisation – write a list of the conditions under which you think each works and does not work. Does any one method come out as superior or inferior in your list? If so, try to explain why.

Review exercise

Evaluation

In summary, attempts to reduce discrimination and prejudice have met with varying levels of success, no one strategy simply applied works over a longer period of time. A person's social identity and how self-categorisation takes place are fundamental to being human and living in a complex society. Changing identities, attitudes and behaviour is hard once they have become strongly established. To be successful strategies should take account of research findings by social psychologists.

Two extensions of recent theory and research in relation to prejudice and discrimination are provided in Chapter 6. These are terror management theory and everyday communications. These two different extensions provide up-to-date thinking in the area. You may wish to dip into one or both of them upon completion of reading this chapter.

Summary

Social psychologists have studied prejudice and discrimination for over 100 years; the most influential and important approach has been one looking at relationships between social groups. Racism and sexism are common examples: 'new racism' is evidenced by denial of discrimination, annoyance that minorities ask for equal treatment, and resentment at special treatment. Stereotypes play an important role since they ignore differences between individuals by assuming that all members of a social group share the same or similar characteristics. Stereotyping results from spontaneous thought: encouraging deliberative thought may serve to reduce the tendency to stereotype people.

Sherif's summer camp experiment investigated realistic group conflict by getting two groups to compete against each other. This produced intergroup hostility. The findings have been difficult to replicate.

The minimal group paradigm has been used extensively to explore ingroup favouritism through membership of a social group in the absence of intergroup competition. Social identity theory states that people are motivated to evaluate and understand their social identity and this evaluation is achieved through comparisons with other groups. Self-categorisation theory is an extension of social identity theory. It states that how you categorise yourself in relation to social group membership is of fundamental importance. Individual approaches include the authoritarian personality, and the frustration–aggression hypothesis. Attempts to reduce prejudice and discrimination have been investigated and tried, in relation to setting group superordinate goals, getting individuals of different groups to engage in meaningful contact, and through attempting to get people to recategorise themselves.

Further reading

Aronson, E. (1999) *The Social Animal*, New York: Worth Publishers. One of the classic texts on social psychology that has recently been updated for the 8th edition. Has an excellent chapter on prejudice with a detailed look at the jigsaw method the author pioneered.

Augoustinos, M. and Walker, I. (1995) *Social Cognition: An Integrated Approach*, London: Sage Publications. Has a well-informed chapter on social identity and another chapter on prejudice stereotypes and attributions. The attributional approach is useful since the chapter above does not deal with this.

Brown, R. (1995) *Prejudice: Its Social Psychology*, Oxford: Blackwell. Detailed, readable and up-to-date account of theory, concepts and research. Strong focus on intergroup relationships and social identity theory, but covers other approaches well also. Useful extended chapter on reducing prejudice using the contact hypothesis.

Smith, P. and Harris Bond, M. (1998) *Social Psychology across Cultures*, London: Prentice Hall. Has a very useful chapter on intergroup relations which deals with the wider cultural and intercultural contexts. Also deals with cultural stereotypes.

6

Social cognition
Development, extensions and applications

 Introduction
Social cognition and child development
Extensions
Applications
Summary

Introduction

In this chapter we shall look at a number of selected areas to give you a flavour of how social cognition has been investigated with respect to child development, extended to new theoretical and practical developments with respect to terror management theory and everyday communications, and applied to the contexts of health and sport. We will only 'dip in' to each of these areas, but it is hoped that sufficient information is provided to 'whet your appetite' and so motivate you to explore more fully one or more areas for yourself.

Probably the best way to use this chapter is to regard the three major sections as extensions of the earlier chapters in this book. Hence, pages 128–31, 139–41 and 141–4 on attribution are best read after Chapters 2 and 3; pages 130–31 after Chapter 4; and pages 135–41 after Chapter 5.

Social cognition and child development

We have seen in Chapters 2 and 3 accounts and descriptions of the way people attribute causes to explain social events. The theory and research in these chapters relate to adults, who are quite sophisticated in their causal explanations. It is of interest to discover how children develop as attributors and to plot the patterns that they show. In the first section we will consider attributions and in the second social representations as they develop in children.

Attributional development

Children develop an awareness of causality quite early in their life; for example, Frye (1991) demonstrated that 4- to 8-month-olds were able to discriminate between spatial events (such as objects hitting one another) which were causally related and those which were not. By the age of 3 to 4 years children are conscious of the consequences and causes of their own actions and show motivation in controlling outcomes (Schneider and Unzer, 1992). Understanding of physical causality develops early in life, but applying causality in the social world is more complex, as we shall see.

In Chapters 2 and 3 we saw that Kelley's discounting principle and the fundamental attribution error are important rules that adults use when making causal attributions. What happens in childhood?

Children's use of the discounting principle

Evidence for the use of the discounting principle in childhood seems to be mixed, and there seems to be a tendency for younger children to use the principle for themselves, but not when explaining the behaviour of others (Kassin and Pryor, 1985). What seems most likely is that the discounting principle is used when children have previous experience of a social context and when they are at a certain stage of cognitive development. This was investigated by Kassin and Ellis (1988), using 5–7-year-old and 8–10-year-old children. These children were given previous experience by being rewarded for eating chocolate or tasteless biscuits. The children then watched videotapes of other children in the same situations. The children participants were then asked to decide whether the children they had seen on tape really enjoyed what they had eaten and why. It was found that children who had been given previous experience of being rewarded for eating either chocolate or tasteless biscuits used the discounting principle. Miller and Aloise (1989) found that younger children, 4- to 5-year-olds, used the discounting principle when an external cause was made highly salient. Overall then, evidence exists for the use of discounting, but only under special circumstances – it is not as widely used in children as in adults.

Children's use of the fundamental attribution error

The fundamental attribution error is the pervasive tendency in adults of attributing causes to internal, stable, dispositions rather than external, situational factors. In children this seems to be acquired rather than being automatic, with evidence that the tendency in children is more towards external attributions as the norm (Fiske and Taylor, 1991). Children have to learn that other people are causal agents and hence to make internal attributions to others. One factor which has been established to promote making internal attributions is evaluation. Beauvois (1984) has shown that evaluation of performance (success or failure) at school and behaviour (good or bad) at home serves to focus the attention of children on their own ability and effort. This is reinforced by attributions parents make to their children's behaviour; parents tend to explain a child's conduct in terms of internal or dispositional attributions. Whilst this may be further evidence of adults displaying the fundamental attribution error, the consequence for their children is that it socialises them towards internal, dispositional attributions (Dix *et al.*, 1986).

Children's attributions of success and failure

This leads on to Weiner's model of attribution of success and failure (see Chapter 2). Over the period of 5–13 years it seems that children slowly learn to change their attention from whether the task is easy or difficult in relation to consequent success or failure, to internal attributions. Young children do not distinguish between effort and ability, assuming that success at a difficult task reflects being intelligent. By mid-childhood a relationship is seen between effort, ability and successful outcome (Nesdale and Pope, 1985). As children become teenagers the links between effort and ability and success or failure at school are firmly established. This is summarised in Figure 6.1.

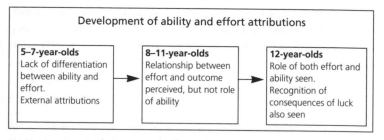

Figure 6.1 **Development of understanding of effort and ability in relation to success and failure in different aged children**

Identify how research by developmental psychologists has shown children to use: the discounting principle; the fundamental attribution error; and children's attribution for success and failure.

Take the example of the fundamental attribution error and ask a 5-year-old child and a 13-year-old teenager to explain why people laugh at a joke. If they say because the joke is funny then an external attribution is being made, if something to do with the person who laughs having a sense of humour then an internal attribution is being made. See if there is a difference in attribution between the two age groups.

Attributional patterns displayed by adults are acquired and learned in childhood, sometimes with childhood patterns being reversed as part of this process. Finally, the culture will also determine the attribution patterns a child acquires, reflecting the individualist–collectivistic distinction made between cultures (Smith and Harris Bond, 1998).

Development of social representations

In Chapter 4 we saw that social representations are ways in which people mentally represent cultural values, beliefs and social norms;

they are shared understandings of our social world (Moscovici, 1981). Much of a child's social development will, therefore, involve learning about the shared understandings of his or her culture. Corsaro (1990) suggests that peer interaction and play in children functions to make adult rules and values familiar and understandable to the child. One function, amongst many, of play is that children jointly construct social representations of how the social world works.

An interesting study into how children of different ages construct their ideas of mental illness was conducted by de Rosa (1987). Using interviews and drawings of children and young adolescents, de Rosa (1987) claimed that the development of social representations of 'mad' paralleled the historical change from organic, brain disorder, to psychological disorder. de Rosa claims that 5- to 6-year-olds represented 'mad' as deviant, criminal, and dangerous in a person. Whilst 8- to 9-year-olds focused on factors outside the person, such as drugs, to represent the causes of madness. Young adolescents used more psychological concepts referring to inner mental processes and disturbed thought. The social representation of 'mad' should then reflect the accepted or prevalent views of the culture in which a person lives.

Ask two groups of children, one group being 5 years of age and the other 10-year-olds, what it means to call a person (grown-up) 'mad'. Analyse responses according to factors inside a person and factors outside a person. You should find that the 10-year-olds focus more on factors outside the person.

Progress exercise

Extensions

In this section we consider two different extensions to the theories and research considered in Chapter 5 on prejudice and discrimination. Each can be read separately, but it would be a good idea to have read Chapter 5 first, or briefly refreshed your memory for the material in that chapter.

Terror management theory: self-esteem and prejudice

We saw in Chapter 5 that self-categorisation theory (Turner, 1985) is required to explain and understand social identity theory. Specifically, it is necessary for an individual to categorise him- or herself as a member of a social group. If the group is positively regarded in society this may maintain or enhance our self-esteem, whilst a negatively regarded group may adversely affect our self-esteem. Two points underlie what is being said here: first, people have a basic need to maintain favourable self-esteem; and second, people have a basic desire to promote the beliefs and values of their own cultural world view, which is often achieved at the expense of other cultural world views. Greenberg *et al.* (1997) ask the question why these two fundamental human motives exist, and have formulated **terror management theory** as an explanation.

Terror management theory starts from the assumption that humans and other animals possess a basic instinct for self-preservation. In humans, however, self-consciousness and the knowledge that one is mortal and will die produces a potential within us all for awe and horror. This is because the basic instinct for self-preservation is negated by our awareness of our mortality. Greenberg *et al.* (1997) then go on to state that people control this terror by creating a culture. Individual identification with, and being part of, a culture, provides order and meaning and has the consequence of making people feel valued and significant. This is the basis of self-esteem, which is then maintained by individuals accepting and promoting their particular culture, as well as showing culturally valued attributes and behaviours. Culture then 'buffers' anxiety or terror through making the individual feel he or she is a valuable member of a world which has meaning.

Greenberg *et al.* (1997) then go on to show how prejudice, discrimination, and intolerance follow as a consequence of terror management theory. A person's cultural world view is both fragile and a social construction of reality; the validity or relevance of the world view is in need of constant affirmation. Hence, the existence of other cultures, religions, values, etc., threatens one's own views. Three general responses, all dismissing other world views, are possible, as shown in Figure 6.2.

Identify aspects of terror management theory that may lead a person to be prejudiced. Identify a prejudice that you hold and see if any of these aspects you have identified apply to you personally.

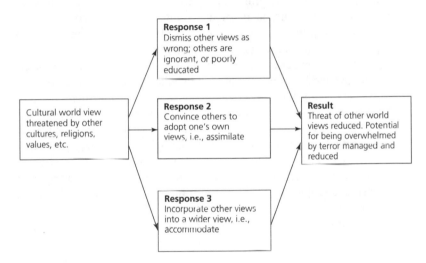

Figure 6.2 **Three responses to management of terror when an individual's world view is threatened**

Terror management theory, therefore, takes account of very important and fundamental human motives to explain how prejudice, discrimination and intergroup conflict are such prevalent and enduring aspects of human social and cultural life. Producing a theory is one thing, the next step is to look for empirical support. One way Greenberg *et al.* (1997) have done this is through experiments based on what they call the **mortality salience hypothesis**. This is characterised as follows:

if a psychological structure provides protection against potential terror from mortality, reminding people of their mortality should increase the need for protection for the structure.

(Greenberg *et al.* 1997)

This should result in protection of the cultural world view and seeking to reassure one's self-worth. For example, most people who live in a democratic society hold the election of their government very dear to their hearts and regard democracy as the best way to have a country governed. Making people aware of their mortality should result in such people defending more strongly the value they place on democracy and the need for all countries to have democratically elected governments. Greenberg *et al.* (1997) cite over forty studies producing evidence to support this hypothesis.

The basic experimental paradigm that is used by these researchers is to give participants, who are led to believe that they are taking part in a personality study, a personality questionnaire, together with some open-ended questions to complete. The open-ended questions ask participants to write a few sentences about what they think will happen to them when they die, and the thoughts and emotions they experience when asked to consider their own death. Participants in the control condition complete the same personality questionnaire, but are given open-ended questions on neutral topics such as eating a meal at a restaurant. Participants in both the mortality salience and control conditions are subsequently asked to make judgements about others who either threaten or support their own world views.

Greenberg *et al.* (1990) found that Christians rated other Christians more positively and Jews more negatively in the mortality salience condition. Harman-Jones *et al.* (1996) report a general increase in liking for the ingroup, and decrease in liking for the outgroup. For example, fans of a football team will show increased liking for fans of the same team, but increased rivalry and dislike of fans of another team. These researchers also found ingroup bias intensified in the minimal group paradigm of Tajfel (see Chapter 5). This means that greater favouritism and preference is given to the group that you are a member of, with another group that you are not a member of being treated more unfairly. Figure 6.3 summarises the effects of increasing awareness of mortality on need for self-esteem and one's cultural world view.

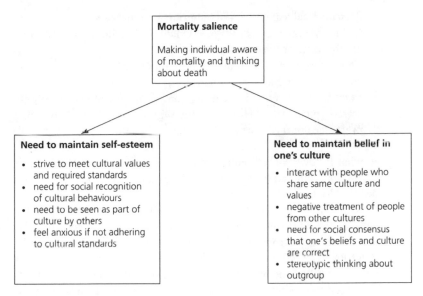

Figure 6.3 **Consequences of mortality salience on need to maintain self-esteem and belief in correctness of one's own culture and associated values**
Source: **Adapted from Greenberg *et al.*, 1997**

Terror management theory offers an interesting approach to prejudice and intergroup conflict based on fundamental human needs. To date the theory has been less valuable in suggesting ways of reducing prejudice, discrimination and conflict. Indeed, it seems to suggest, rather depressingly, that these are inevitable consequences of human culture.

Prejudice and everyday communications

Ruscher (1998) investigated and analysed how ingroup members actually talk about outgroup members. Ruscher's research is experimental in nature but has good ecological validity since analysis of actual conversations between pairs of people discussing outgroups and individuals representing outgroups has been conducted. Consistent with some of the claims made in Chapter 5, when we looked at stereotyping, four main findings have emerged when ingroups talk about outgroups. These are:

1 Stereotypical aspects of the outgroup are emphasised.
2 Outgroup homogeneity (all individuals belonging to the outgroup are the same or very similar) is present.
3 The outgroup and its individual members are seen as lacking in competence and less intelligent.
4 Ingroup members characterise outgroup members in highly stereotypical ways. However, the ingroup members deny being prejudiced or try to justify their views.

In what follows we will consider some of the evidence that Ruscher (1998) has gathered to substantiate these claims, but space prevents a detailed look at each.

Ruscher and Hammer (1994) conducted a study to investigate the consequences for stereotypical conversation when somebody initially seen to be an ingroup member is found out to be a member of an outgroup. The researchers hypothesised that upon discovering that a person is really a member of an outgroup, conversation between dyads will become stereotypical of the outgroup image. Dyads (pairs of people) received two sets of information, one consistent with an alcoholic stereotype, and the other inconsistent. Half of the dyads were told from the outset that the person was an alcoholic, whilst the other half received this information after forming an initial impression. This latter condition was called the 'disrupted impression'. After the dyads had engaged in conversation about the person, analysis was conducted on the amount of time spent in stereotype-consistent discussion and the number of negative stereotype comments made. As can be seen from Figure 6.4, dyads in 'disrupted' conditions both spent more time in and made more stereotype-consistent comments compared to stereotype-inconsistent comments. This provides support for Ruscher and Hammer's hypothesis stated earlier.

Linguistic ingroup bias

Maas and Acuri (1996) found evidence, from conversational analysis using a research design similar to that above, for what they called the **linguistic ingroup bias**. This summarises the findings that when ingroup members are talking about outgroup members, who behave in expected ways, they are referred to in more abstract terms (for example, describing someone as aggressive when told that the person

(a)

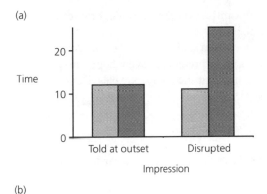

(b)

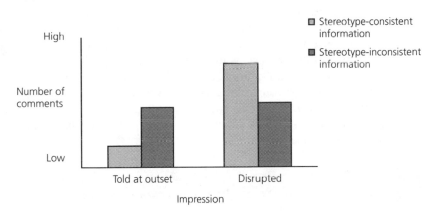

Figure 6.4 **Time spent discussing stereotype-consistent and inconsistent information in the two experimental conditions (a); number of stereotype-consistent and inconsistent comments in the two conditions (b)**
Source: Adapted from Ruscher and Hammer, 1994

gently slapped someone in the face). By contrast, unexpected outgroup behaviours are referred to in more concrete or specific language (for example, correctly answering a certain quiz question rather than being intelligent). The importance and significance of the linguistic ingroup bias is that stereotypically-consistent or expected outgroup behaviour is described at an abstract level, hence confirming the stereotype. Whereas stereotypically-inconsistent or unexpected out-group behaviour is described at a concrete level, and so does not challenge the general stereotype. This bias can be reduced when an instruction is given to concentrate on the individual rather than the group he or she is a member of.

Ruscher (1998) has found, from analysing dyadic conversation, that people make efforts not to appear prejudiced even though they display outgroup stereotyping and the linguistic intergroup bias. Denial is often indicated through phrases such as:

'I have nothing against them, but . . .'

'Some of my best friends are Y, however, this particular Y . . .'

Such expressions serve to maintain the outgroup stereotype, but are used by the individual in an attempt to manage the impression he or she makes with others (Kunda and Oleson, 1995). People may attempt to 'mask' their prejudice by, for example, using negative-stereotype irrelevant information to show to others that these negative views do not derive from general prejudiced attitudes. Finally, prejudice may be masked by a person making positive verbal remarks about an outgroup member, but at the same time engaging in negative non-verbal behaviour (such as avoiding eye-contact, or orienting their body away from the other person).

Progress exercise

Identify the four main findings from Ruscher's research on stereotyping when ingroups talk about outgroups. Identify an ingroup your friend is a member of and engage him/her in a discussion about an outgroup (for example, if your friend supports the home football team, ask him to talk about the visiting away team). See if you can spot the four categories identified by Ruscher in how your friend talks about the outgroup.

In summary, analysis of everyday communications between two people reveals differential use of language for ingroups and outgroups that serves to maintain a prejudicial stereotype. Furthermore, people attempt to deny holding prejudicial attitudes.

Extensions

Attribution and health

In Chapter 2 when evaluating concepts and models of attribution we noted that the abnormal conditions model of Hilton and Slugoski (1986) states that people only really make efforts to give causal explanations when an abnormal event happens. In the context of ill health, a diagnosis of a serious condition such as cancer, being HIV positive, heart attack, etc. should fulfil the abnormal conditions model. This is supported from research by Turnquist *et al.* (1988) who report that between 69 and 95 per cent of patients report illness-related attributions. This was found to vary according to severity of the illness, and length of time since being first diagnosed. Causal attributions become more important to people sometime after initial diagnosis, rather than at the time of initial diagnosis. For example, Taylor *et al.* (1984) found that only 28 per cent of women initially diagnosed as having breast cancer were concerned with causal explanations. However, after a few months, and during recovery from treatment, this rose to over 40 per cent. Such a finding may reflect the preoccupations at the time: upon initial diagnosis women are more concerned with treatment, prognosis and survival. After a number of months, during recovery, initial concerns have been allayed and the preoccupation is now more to do with controlling and maintaining recovery. This may be facilitated by attributing causes, especially when the causes are within the person's control. If people with serious illness perceive a degree of self-control that they have over their illness this may have a positive effect on how well they are able to adjust to the illness or condition (Thompson, 1981). This brings to mind Weiner's (1979, 1986) model of success and failure which we looked at in some detail in Chapter 2.

Murray and McMillan (1989) investigated people's lay explanations of cancer amongst 60 adults of varying age, social class, and sex. Attributions provided by these adults were coded into the eight categories suggested by Weiner (1986) – see Figure 2.6. Over 200 causal attributions were classified into these categories; Figure 6.5 gives percentages for the four most frequently used categories.

As can be seen, the most commonly used category was the internal and controllable one – this implies that personal effort can have a

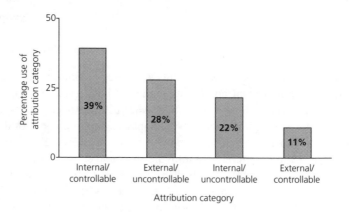

Figure 6.5 **Lay explanations of cancer in relation to Weiner's (1986) attribution model**
Source: **Adapted from Murray and McMillan, 1989**

positive effect on 'beating the big C'. The second most frequently cited category was that of external and uncontrollable: here cancer patients are making chance and luck attributions about their ability to survive the disease. The third most frequently cited category was that of internal and uncontrollable; this may reflect a person accepting responsibility for their cancer and being able to adjust to the disease but feeling that they may only have a limited influence on the condition. The final category of external/controllable reflects confidence in help from others (doctors, nurses, care-giver, etc.) to recover from the disease. Interestingly, Murray and McMillan (1989) found that older people were more likely to attribute the cause of cancer to external and uncontrollable events – reflecting perhaps a more fatalistic approach to being able to do anything about their illness.

Actor–observer differences and health

Actor–observer differences have also been investigated by health psychologists. Turnquist *et al.* (1988) report that actors (the patient or ill person) tend to make situational or external attributions for the illness. In contrast, observers, particularly those who may provide care for the person, tend to attribute to the person, thus making dispositional or internal attributions. The situational or external tendency for attribution by the sick person may reflect self-protection (see Chapter 3) and not taking responsibility for their illness. This may have the consequence of the person making a poor adjustment. The type of attributions made by the observer may relate to the level of care that they would be willing to provide. For example, Brewin (1984) found that medical students, in a simulated study, were more willing to prescribe antidepressants or tranquillisers when they perceived a patient's causes to result from uncontrollable events.

Identify the different attributions made by the sick person and a person caring for the sick person. Now think of a recent time when you were ill, for example, with the 'flu. Write down how you attribute the causes of your illness and then ask someone who looked after you (parent, etc.) to make attributions as to the cause of your illness. Do you notice any actor–observer differences in line with research?

Progress exercise

In summary, establishing how people and their care-givers attribute causes for illness may affect the amount of effort both will give when trying to overcome the illness or disease. Attribution theory provides important insights in the health context.

Attribution and sport

Sport offers a good application of attribution theory since most people play sport, albeit at different levels, and there are usually winners and losers. How athletes explain causes for winning or losing is of interest in itself, but is also likely to have important consequences for future performance and expectations. Here we will look at differences in attributions for success and failure, measuring causal dimensions, attributional training and gender differences.

Motivation, self-confidence and self-esteem are of critical importance for athletic performance (Cox, 1998). How an athlete feels about his or her success will, in part, depend on whether an internal or external (see Chapter 2) attribution is made. McAuley *et al.* (1983)

provided a relationship between attributions, outcome and affect, as shown in Figure 6.6.

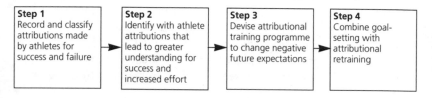

Step 1	Step 2	Step 3	Step 4
Record and classify attributions made by athletes for success and failure	Identify with athlete attributions that lead to greater understanding for success and increased effort	Devise attributional training programme to change negative future expectations	Combine goal-setting with attributional retraining

Figure 6.6 **Four-step model of attributional retraining to change dysfunctional attribution patterns**
Source: **Adapted from Cox, 1998**

As can be seen, attributing success to internal causes (an athlete's skills, ability, experience, etc.) leads to feelings of pride, confidence and perception of competence. On the other hand, attributing failure or losing to internal causes (lack of skills, no ability, etc.) leads to feelings of shame, incompetence, and depression. In the former situation, self-esteem, self-confidence and motivation will be enhanced, and in the latter these will be reduced. Enhancing self-esteem and self-confidence is likely to lead to high levels of performance in the future and further success. Athletes who lose are more likely to search for causal explanations than those who win, especially if the athlete lost when he or she expected to win (Biddle and Hill, 1992).

The causal dimension scale for measuring attributions

A widely used scale for measuring causal attributions is based on a modification of Weiner's (1979, 1986) model of success and failure (see Chapter 2, pages 24–6). The original dimensions of internal–external, and stable–unstable are retained. However, the controllable–uncontrollable dimension is split into two dimensions. These are external control and personal control; the former concerns causes controlled by other people (in sport this may be other members of the team, the referee, etc.) and the latter causes within the control of the individual. McAuley *et al.* (1992) have used these four dimensions to develop the **Causal Dimension Scale**. This scale consists of 3 items related to each of the four dimensions where each item is scored on a 9-point scale. An example from the personal control dimension is shown below.

Is the cause something you can regulate?						Is the cause something you cannot regulate?		
9	8	7	6	5	4	3	2	1

Hence, each of the four dimensions can be measured on a range of 3 to 27, where higher values indicate more internal, stable, uncontrollable by others, and controllable by self-attributions.

The causal dimension scale is very useful for measuring how athletes attribute causes for success and failure and also provides information that may be of use in **attributional retraining**. For example, an athlete with a track record of winning should make a stable attribution reflecting skill, ability, and experience. However, if the same athlete loses on an occasion he or she should attribute to unstable causes since previous history has been one of success. Unstable causes may be playing conditions, poor refereeing, having an off-day, etc. This attributional pattern will maintain high self-esteem and self-confidence, resulting in positive expectations for the future. By contrast, consider an athlete with low self-esteem, a history of losing at a sport, who makes internal, stable and uncontrollable attributions along the line 'I'm no good at this sport' or 'I do not have the ability to learn this sport'. This person would expect to fail in the future and feel he or she lacks the confidence to master the skills of the sport. Attributional retraining is aimed at changing causal attribution patterns to result in athletes feeling they can succeed and can master the skills. Research has shown that attributional retraining is more effective with children than adults in terms of influencing future expectations and self-esteem (Rudisill, 1988). This does not mean that such retraining is ineffective with adults. This research has led to a four-step model of attributional retaining which is summarised in Figure 6.7.

Think back to two occasions when you last played a sport you enjoyed – one should be where you won and the other where you lost. Write down the causes you perceive for both winning and losing on those different occasions. Is there a pattern of attributing success to internal causes and failure to external causes? What attributional retraining might be appropriate for you and why?

Progress exercise

		Outcome	
		Success	**Failure**
Attribution	**Internal**	Pride Confidence Competence Satisfaction	Guilt Shame Incompetence Depression
	External	Gratitude Thankfulness Luck	Anger Surprise Astonishment

Figure 6.7 **Affective consequences of internal or external attributions for success and failure in sport**
Source: **Adapted from McAuley et al., 1983**

Finally, mixed evidence has been produced to suggest that male and female athletes differ in the extent to which they exhibit the self-serving bias (see Chapter 3, pages 48–50). White (1993) showed that males exhibit the self-serving bias more than females; meaning that males use more self-enhancement attributions to boost self-esteem and expectation for success. Hendy and Boyer (1993) showed that females place more importance on personal controllable factors such as diet and mental state; however, research findings are generally conflicting about such male and female attribution differences.

In summary, attribution theory together with biases and errors help us to understand how athletes attribute causes for their success or failure. Dysfunctional attribution patterns can be changed through attributional retraining.

Summary

Adult patterns of causal attribution are learned in childhood: however, in some cases of error and bias the pattern may be reversed as with the fundamental attribution error. Collectivist and individualistic cultures influence how the child develops attributions. Social representations develop in childhood from shared understandings of the culture into which they are socialised and develop. Play may serve a function of children jointly constructing shared representations.

Terror management theory attempts to explain prejudice and intergroup conflict, based on the fundamental needs a person has for self-preservation and self-esteem. Individual identification with a culture provides meaning and self-value and helps manage the potential terror of mortality.

Analysis of everyday communications made between two people indicates that people use different language when referring to an ingroup and an outgroup. The language differences serve to maintain prejudiced stereotypes.

Understanding how people attribute causes to their illness helps predict whether people will make an effort to recover and how well they adjust to the condition. Weiner's model of success and failure has been applied to the health context. Evidence for actor (patient) and observer (care-giver) bias has also been found. Success or failure in sport has been investigated from an attributional perspective. Attributing success to internal causes leads to confidence and prediction of future success; attributing failure to external causes also enhances self-esteem. Opposite attributions to these may be dysfunctional and require attribution of retraining.

Further reading

Cox, R. H. (1998) *Sport psychology: Concepts and Applications*, Boston, MA: McGraw-Hill.
Good, accessible, and readable, introductory text covering general area of sport psychology. Two chapters focus specifically on the social psychology of sport, with one dealing exclusively with attribution across a range of individual and team sports.

Durkin, K. (1995) *Developmental Social Psychology: From Infancy to Old Age*, Oxford: Blackwell.
Highly regarded and readable text on social development. Has three chapters devoted to social cognition: one deals quite fully with attribution; another gives some consideration to social representations in childhood.

Greenberg, J., Solomon, S. and Pyszczynski, T. (1997) Terror Management Theory of self-esteem and cultural world views. In M. P. Zanna (ed.), *Advances in Experimental Social Psychology*, vol. 29, San Diego, CA: Academic Press.

Advanced reading and should only be dipped into to get a better sense of theory and research in this area. Not an accessible, easy to read text, or summary article on this fascinating new area of development.

Murray, M. (1990) Lay representations of illness. In P. Bennett, J. Weinman and P. Spurgeon (eds), *Current Developments in Health Psychology*, London: Harwood Academic Publishers.
Useful chapter summarising theory and empirical research on both attribution and social representations in a health context. Quite accessible, if a little too summarised in places.

7

Study aids

IMPROVING YOUR ESSAY WRITING SKILLS

At this point in the book you have acquired the knowledge necessary to tackle the exam itself. Answering exam questions is a skill, and in this chapter we hope to help you improve this skill. A common mistake that some students make is not providing the kind of evidence the examiner is looking for. Another is failing to answer the question properly despite providing lots of information. Typically, a grade C answer is accurate and reasonably constructed, but has limited detail and commentary. To lift such an answer to an A or B grade may require no more than fuller detail, better use of material and a coherent organisation. By studying the essays below, and the comments that follow, you can learn how to turn your grade C answer into a grade A. Please note that marks given by the examiner in the practice essays should be used as a guide only, and are not definitive. They represent the 'raw marks' given by an AQA/AEB examiner – that is, the marks the examiner would give to the examining board based on a total of 24 marks per question broken down into Skill A (description) and Skill B (evaluation). A table showing this scheme is in Appendix C of Paul Humphreys' title in this series *Exam Success in AEB Psychology*. They may not be the marks given on the examination certificate received ultimately by the student because all examining boards are required to use a common standardised system called the Uniform Mark Scale (UMS) which adjusts all raw scores to a single standard acceptable to all examining boards.

The essays are about the length a student would be able to write in 35–40 minutes (leaving extra time for planning and checking). Each essay is followed by detailed comments about its strengths and weaknesses. The most common problems to look for are:

- Students frequently fail to answer the actual question set, and present 'one they made earlier' (the *Blue Peter* answer).
- Many weak essays suffer from a lack of evaluation or commentary.
- On the other hand students sometimes go too far in the other direction and their essays are all evaluation. Description is vital in demonstrating your knowledge and understanding of the selected topic.
- Don't write 'everything you know' in the hope that something will get credit. Excellence is displayed through selectivity; therefore improvements can often be made by *removing* material which is irrelevant to the question set.

For more ideas about how to write good essays you should consult *Exam Success in AEB Psychology* (in this series) by Paul Humphreys.

Practice essay 1

(a) **Describe the main characteristics of social identity theory. (12 marks)**

(b) **Assess the value of social identity theory as an explanation of social perception. (12 marks)**

[AEB Summer 1998]

Starting point: Questions with sub-sections are intended to help give structure to your essay. They also often specify how you should present your evaluative material. In this case you are asked to evaluate social identity theory insofar as it can explain the process of social perception. You should ensure that you do this rather than a more generalised evaluation of the theory.

Forty-five minutes is allowed for this question. You should allocate roughly the same amount of time to (a) and (b); however, (b) is more demanding since you are required to evaluate and you may wish to devote a little more time to this sub-section of the question.

Candidate's answer

(a) Social identity theory was developed by Tajfel to explain how we interact with our peers and social groups, and how we come to form opinions of ourselves. Tajfel's theory suggests that we all hold an image of ourselves and we make this image a positive one as much as possible. This is done by our self-evaluation, Tajfel suggested that we concentrate on what we see as positive characteristics and from these we form our own identity.

From this, Tajfel claimed that we adapt our self-image to fit in with our different social groups, so we can concentrate on different aspects of our personality depending on which social group we are with, fitting into each group. It could be said that this is conforming, a concept Crutchfield described as 'yielding to group pressure'. However Tajfel put forward the idea that it is not only our self-image which is manipulated. He also claimed in the social identity theory that we attribute the positive aspects of our own personality to the members of our social group – thus giving them a positive image in our eyes. This in turn means that we have a positive image of ourselves because we are part of this ingroup.

This same sort of stereotyping occurs when what we see as negative stereotypes in that we attribute negative characteristics to those groups that we don't belong to (the outgroup). Tajfel suggested that it is these generalisations and the attribution of our behaviour to social groups which moulds our social behaviour.

Tajfel suggested that the main reason for this behaviour was the concept of self-esteem. We want to have a positive self-image, and so to do this we attribute positive characteristics to ourselves and our social groups to give us self-esteem and self-confidence. We further our self-esteem by giving negative characteristics to members of the groups to which we don't belong.

Tajfel states that it is on these generalised perceptions of others and our own groups that our social groups are based. We identify with those groups with which we feel that we share common characteristics.

(b) Social identity theory can be used to explain the processes of social perception. For example, Tajfel did a study himself using Bristol schoolboys. The boys had to estimate how many dots there were in a picture and those who were 'overestimators' were placed in one group while the 'underestimators' were in a different group. At least that is what the boys thought. In fact they were put in these groups just randomly. Their next task was to give out points to all the boys in the groups. At the end of the experiment each boy would receive money for the points they got. Tajfel found that the boys gave more points to people who were in their group and fewer to those in the other group. This therefore supports social identity theory.

There are several criticisms of this study. It just used schoolboys and therefore was a biased group. It took place in a laboratory and therefore lacked ecological validity. The boys were in a situation where they were forced to behave this way. This is called demand characteristics.

Another study by Turner (1975) found that when schoolboys were given the chance they preferred to reward themselves rather than their group. This shows that the self-serving bias is stronger that the group-serving bias.

Another famous study also looked at the behaviour of boys. This study was conducted by Sherif. The boys all went to a summer camp and were put in two groups, the Rattlers and the Eagles. When they had to compete against the other group they showed a lot of prejudice against them. Prejudice is an example of a social behaviour which can be explained by social identity theory. The boys also had to play a game and behaved in a similar fashion to the boys in Tajfel's study.

One problem with social identity theory is that it may not apply to all cultures. It may be relevant to White European, middle-class, schoolboys but not other people. So it is not a universal theory of behaviour.

Examiner's comments

Part (a) is repetitive. What does the candidate actually say? The ingroup is given positive characteristics and this increases our sense of self-esteem. The outgroup is given negative characteristics and this also increases our sense of self-esteem. These processes are fundamental to social behaviour. Thus the answer is limited. It is accurate and shows a good understanding of social identity theory, which makes it better than basic, muddled and flawed. A mark of 5 out of 12 would be appropriate.

How could the candidate have improved this? By reference to examples of ingroup and outgroup identity; by the use of more specialist terms such as ingroup favouritism; by consideration of concepts such as the illusion of outgroup homogeneity. All of this would provide a sense of greater depth (detail) and breadth to the essay, as well as communicating understanding. This answer makes one feel that the candidate only has a very thin grasp on the concept.

Part (b) has an excellent start by framing the question to remind the writer what they should write about. The choice of Tajfel's study is obvious but it is not necessary to provide quite this amount of detail. Time would have been better spent explaining exactly how this study does support social identity theory. The next paragraph offers some evaluations of the study but these lack elaboration and thus seem rather rote learned instead of giving a perceptive analysis of the study. Nonetheless they show some critical awareness.

The candidate goes on to present other relevant pieces of evidence which all lend support to the theory. The response is much more readable than for Part (a) and this sense of organisation is rewarded in the mark. It is also much better informed than Part (a). A good description of Part (b) is 'reasonable though slightly limited, effective use of material and some evidence of coherent elaboration'. A mark of 8 out of 12 is appropriate since there is a reasonable but limited use of material together with some evaluation.

An overall mark of 13 out of 24 awarded, the equivalent of a grade C. You can see that the mark would have been considerably improved by more detail in Part (a). This candidate could even have got a grade A!

Practice essay 2

Discuss explanations of *two* attributional biases (e.g. the fundamental attribution error and the self-serving bias). (24 marks)
[AEB Summer 1999]

Starting point: This is a very straightforward question which clearly requests you to describe and evaluate two attributional biases. Should you know more than two you might use the others to evaluate the two you describe. Candidates often find it difficult to avoid using the examples given but they are there for guidance only and you can choose any biases.

An important thing to note is that the question asks for

'explanations' rather than just a description of the biases. A good answer must ensure that the biases are explained *rather than just defined. In addition you are asked to discuss, which means you also need to evaluate the biases you choose to write about.*

Candidate's answer

Attribution theory explains the processes of interpreting the causes of observed behaviour. There are two types of causes: internal and external. Internal or dispositional causes are those explanations which are based on personal attributes. For example, you might explain why someone was late because they were always late and it was an aspect of their personality. External attributions are when you explain your own or someone else's behaviour as having been caused by something outside themselves. For example, you might explain the reason for someone's lateness as being due to a late bus.

There have been several theories of attribution. Kelley's covariation model proposed that attributions are made on the basis of three factors: consensus (whether others share the same opinion), consistency (how often a person behaves in the same way) and distinctiveness (the extent to which someone behaves differently from others). Kelley suggested that you could predict someone's behaviour using these three factors. If distinctiveness and consistency are low and consistency is high then internal attributions are likely to be made.

Kelley later revised this model and called the new one the 'causal schemata' theory. He found that people didn't always use the information as he had predicted and that other factors influenced them, such as multiple necessary causes (a group of behaviour all have to be present in order for an attribution to be made) and multiple sufficient causes (any one of several behaviours will be sufficient to create an attribution). This revised theory was more consistent with the observation that attributions are in fact made using minimal amounts of material.

This desire to be a 'cognitive miser' leads to various biases. Two of these will be considered here: the fundamental attribution error (FAE) and the actor–observer effect.

The FAE is that situational factors are likely to be ignored when explaining the behaviour of others. Instead people tend to prefer to make dispositional attributions. For example, when someone is late we tend to suspect that this is a character trait rather than because something happened on the way to school. In the same way that in social cognition we are more likely to seek information to support our own perceptions we are more likely to ignore information that contradicts our cognition. The same principle underlies the FAE. We are less aware of situational factors when observing another's behaviour and therefore prefer to explain their behaviour (to ourselves) in terms of personality or disposition. This helps boost our self-esteem because we can't feel to blame for our own actions. It also makes our cognitive process more efficient because we can make judgements without thinking.

Ross *et al.* conducted a study which showed that the FAE is true. They conducted a quiz and asked observers to rate the general knowledge of the questioners and answerers. They rated the questioners as more knowledgeable even though they knew that they had made up the questions so would inevitably do better.

Some people have criticised the FAE because it doesn't always happen. If you know someone well then you are less likely to make the FAE. If something is very important you are more likely to make the FAE.

The actor–observer bias is similar to the FAE because it also is related to how we interpret the behaviour of another in terms of internal and external attributions. If you are asked to explain the behaviour of an 'actor' you are more likely to refer to situational attributions whereas if you are asked to explain the same behaviour but from the viewpoint of an observer then you would use internal attributions. Part of the reason for using external attributions is that we are more aware of the context and situation surrounding our own action and we presume that is true for any individual.

A laboratory study which demonstrated this actor–observer effect was conducted by Nisbett *et al.* They asked participants to explain for themselves and a friend the reasons for selecting a particular course of study. People tended to give self-explanations which were situational (e.g. what the course has to offer) whereas attributions about others was dispositional (e.g. the course suited their interest in artistic things).

There are other biases as well such as self-serving bias. All of these help us to understand the typical ways that people make attributions. However, these may not be universal. There is evidence that people in other countries don't act the same way. For example, in India people are more aware of situational constraints and therefore are more likely to make external attributions for others. Also if you know someone well this will alter the kind of attribution you make.

Examiner's comments

Many candidates find it difficult to resist giving you 'everything they know about attribution', as is the case here. The candidate has a reasonable knowledge of theories of attribution and cannot resist presenting this material even though it is not directly relevant to this question. The material on theory might have been used effectively as a means of assessing the biases but the candidate hasn't really done that here. Therefore it gains almost no credit. This should remind you that it is imperative that you *answer the question which was set*.

Despite the poor start to this essay, as a whole it is well constructed and the second half is relevant and detailed. The candidate communicates a reasonable understanding of two biases and uses empirical evidence to assess their validity. The candidate does also try to *explain* rather than just describe the biases. Empirical studies have been used well to support the biases, and other commentary introduced as a means of assessing the value of these explanations. There is a tendency to just place the material in the essay rather than using it as effectively as it could be. At the end there is a brief and slightly elaborated consideration of cultural and individual differences.

Overall the descriptive part of this essay is reasonably well-detailed and there is increasing evidence of both breadth and depth. However the descriptions/explanations of both biases tend towards being limited rather than slightly limited.

The evaluative component is again reasonable but limited. There are two studies plus two other paragraphs of commentary. There is some evidence of elaboration but the candidate could have provided, for example, more commentary about what the studies demonstrated.

This essay would receive 8 marks for description and 6 for evaluation, with an overall a mark of 14 out of 24 awarded, which is equivalent to a good C or just a B grade.

KEY RESEARCH SUMMARIES

Article 1

Brown, R. J. (1978) Divided we fall: an analysis of relations between sections of a factory workforce. In H. Tajfel (ed.), *Differentiation between Social Groups: Studies in the Social Psychology of Intergroup Relations,* **London: Academic Press.**

Background

This field study demonstrates an application of both the minimal group paradigm and social identity theory that we considered in Chapter 5. It is a widely cited study in modern texts and regarded as a good example of applied research on issues of great importance to the people concerned.

Introduction

Rupert Brown gained access to an aircraft engineering factory in which he focused on three groups of key workers: production, development and toolroom workers. These three groups had not been getting on that well prior to Brown going into the factory, and this partly centred around relative wage levels for each group of workers. The toolroom workers were the highest paid with the production and development workers paid about the same. The toolroom workers were keen to maintain or enhance the wage differential that presently existed, whilst the other two groups attempted to improve their pay relative to the toolroom workers. In terms of social identity theory ingroups and outgroups had developed.

AIMS OF THE STUDY

The study had three main aims:

1 To demonstrate that the minimal group paradigm of Tajfel is applicable in an applied setting.
2 To demonstrate ingroup and outgroup behaviour using this paradigm.
3 To discover whether superordinate goals helped to reduce intergroup tensions.

METHOD

The three groups of workers were presented with a matrix designed to measure intergroup differentiation in wages. This is shown in Figure 7.1 below. Interviews were also conducted with selected workers and shop stewards from each group.

Groups of workers	Wages				
Toolroom workers	£69.30	£68.80	£68.30	£67.80	£67.30
Production and development workers	£70.30	£69.30	£68.30	£67.30	£66.30

Figure 7.1 **Wages matrix used by Brown (1978) with the three groups of workers in the engineering factory**

Workers were asked to imagine a situation where management had just announced that 10 per cent of the workforce across the whole factory had to be made redundant. This was designed to represent a threat to all workers and hence be regarded as a superordinate situation.

RESULTS

With respect to responses to the wage matrix shown in Figure 7.1, Brown found that the toolroom workers had the overriding aim of maintaining the largest differential between themselves and the other two groups of workers. This was shown by them choosing the extreme right wage column (£67.30:£66.30).

Second, in relation to the redundancy situation, less than 20 per cent of the workers across all three groups wanted to develop a joint strategy and work together in the face of a common threat. Instead, most wanted to protect their own group of workers and let other groups suffer redundancies.

DISCUSSION

The toolroom workers wanted to maintain the differential whatever the cost. This meant that instead of accepting the highest wage shown in the matrix in Figure 7.1 they opted for the lowest wage. This represents rejecting £2.00 per week more since to accept the highest absolute wage for themselves also meant the differential not only disappeared but that the other two groups of workers would be earning more than them. In the end status through wage differential was more important than the best wage possible. This finding represents a good demonstration of both the minimal group paradigm and the claims of social identity theory.

The superordinate situation of redundancy facing the three groups of workers was approached by most in each group saying the other groups should take the cuts in jobs. This finding questions the general claim that superordinate tasks help groups to co-operate. In this situation tensions between the three groups might have increased if the redundancy situation had been real rather than imaginary.

DISCUSSION QUESTIONS

1 To what extent do you think that the different groups of workers regarded the wage matrix, shown in Figure 7.1, as realistic, as it was presented to them?
2 What differences can you identify between the superordinate situation of redundancy presented here and the superordinate tasks Sherif presented to the boys at summer camp (See Chapter 5, pages 118–19)?
3 Imagine you were conducting interviews with the workers about the imaginary redundancy situation? What questions might you ask?
4 How good an application of the minimal group paradigm do you think was made in this study? Identify how this could have been improved.
5 This study was conducted over twenty years ago. What differences in industrial relationships might need to be taken into account if you wished to replicate the study now?

Article 2

Gilbert, D. T., Pelham, B. W. and Krull, D. S. (1988) On cognitive busyness: when person perceivers meet persons perceived, *Journal of Personality and Social Psychology*, 54, 733–40.

Background

The background to this frequently cited study is that it tests the final stage of the three stage model of attribution suggested by Gilbert *et al.* (1988). This model seeks to explain how we arrive at a dispositional attribution and when situational factors are taken into account. The three stages of the model are that we first categorise another person's behaviour (i.e. decide what it is about). Second, the behaviour is characterised (i.e. used to infer specific dispositional traits), and third, the attribution is corrected to take account of situational factors that might be present. In some senses the first two stages can be seen as spontaneous attributions and the third as deliberative (see Chapter 2, pages 14–16).

Introduction

The three stage model of attribution suggested by Gilbert *et al.* (1988) was tested through the use of the idea of cognitive busyness. This was operationalised by having participants engage in a distraction task of reciting interview topics whilst watching a videotape about which they subsequently had to make causal attributions. The hypothesis tested concerned the correction stage of the three-stage model and was as follows:

Participants kept cognitively busy would fail to adequately take situational factors into account, compared to participants not kept cognitively busy, when making causal attributions.

The research represents an extension and deeper understanding of Jones and Davis' correspondent inference model of attribution (see Chapter 2, pages 16–19).

METHOD

College students were recruited to be participants in an experiment in which they watched a silent videotape of a woman in discussion with another person (who was not shown on the tape). The woman fidgeted and displayed various types of restless behaviour, designed to convey the impression that the woman was anxious.

Participants were first divided into two groups where one group was told that the woman was discussing a mundane subject such as holidays, and the other group was told that the woman was discussing her sexual fantasies. Half of the participants in each of these two groups were kept 'cognitively busy' by having to recite interview topics, whilst the other half were not given a distractor task.

This experiment is a 2 × 2 (woman's topic of discussion × cognitively busy) independent measures design, reflecting different participants in each of the four conditions. The main dependent variable was the degree of anxiety that the participants attributed to the woman on the videotape. This was measured using an eleven-point scale, where a high figure indicates a high level of anxiety.

RESULTS

Non-distracted participants rated the woman as highly dispositionally anxious when discussing a mundane topic such as holidays, and much less dispositionally anxious when discussing her sexual fantasies. By contrast, participants made cognitively busy made similar attributions about the woman's dispositional anxiety for both topics of conversation. This is shown in Figure 7.2.

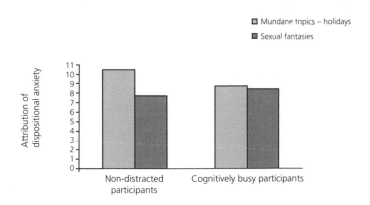

Figure 7.2 **Effects of being cognitively busy on attributions of dispositional anxiety**
Source: **Adapted from Gilbert *et al.*, 1988**

DISCUSSION

The results summarised in Figure 7.2 show that participants who are not distracted or not cognitively busy make corrections for situational factors – in this case, topic of discussion – when making dispositional attributions about anxiety. By contrast, participants who were kept cognitively busy did not take account of different situational factors and made similar attributions about the woman's general state of anxiety.

The results offer support for the three-stage model of attribution and highlight the importance of deliberative thought for taking account of situational factors (external) when making dispositional (internal) attributions.

DISCUSSION QUESTIONS

1 The experimenters assumed that the fidgeting and restless behaviour of the woman on videotape would be interpreted as signs of anxiety. How might you go about checking this?

2 Identify two ways in which the experiment was artificial and think of how you might change the experiment to overcome these types of artificiality.

3 A rating scale was used to measure the anxiety attribution of participants. How might you check to see if participants were using the scale in the same way to reflect similar levels of anxiety?

4 Suppose you only had sufficient participants to conduct a repeated measures design experiment. How would you counterbalance to accommodate this?

5 What further light does this research provide for the correspondent inference model?

Glossary

The first occurrence of each of these terms is highlighted in **bold** type in the main text.

Abnormal condition model proposed by Hilton and Slugoski to account for when people are most likely to make attributions. The model claims that people make attributions when something abnormal or unexpected happens.

Acquiescent response set usually refers to questions or items on a questionnaire which are worded in the same way and where people may show agreement because of this. The presence of an acquiescent response set on a questionnaire usually renders it invalid. An example is the F-scale.

Actor–observer differences are where the actor (self) makes situational or external attributions about his or her behaviour, and attributions about another person's behaviour are dispositional or internal. This differs from the fundamental attribution error which is concerned with dispositional (internal) attributions made about another person's behaviour.

Anchoring and adjustment heuristic is where people make judgements by starting from an initial 'anchor' or point of view and then making adjustment in light of further information. Typically people do not make sufficient adjustment from the original position. See also heuristics of thinking.

Anchoring is a process whereby new information is incorporated into an existing social representation. Not to be confused with the anchoring and adjustment heuristic.

Aschematic traits are traits that are of peripheral or minor importance to a person. Related to peripheral traits, opposite to schematic traits.

Attribution is the process of attempting to determine the causes of our own or other people's behaviour through determining whether the causes are dispositional (internal) or situational (external).

Attributional development concerns understanding how children develop in attributing causes to their own and other people's behaviour. Children tend not to exhibit the fundamental attribution, but this changes as they grow older.

Attributional retraining is offered to athletes who show a dysfunctional attributional style. This is a style where success is attributed to external, uncontrollable causes and failure to poor ability and other internal causes. Attributional retraining seeks to reverse these types of attributions.

Augmenting principle is where a likely cause of behaviour is given greater credence or emphasis when inhibiting or unlikely factors are present. See discounting principle.

Authoritarian personality was first suggested by Adorno to characterise a personality type who is submissive to authority figures, but authoritarian with people lower in status or power. Associated with prejudicial attitudes.

Availability heuristic is a rule of thumb that people use to make a judgement about the frequency of an event. It is based on personal experience and the ease with which the event can be brought mind. See also cognitive miser and heuristics of thinking.

Belief perseverance is where initial beliefs and attitudes are maintained and held on to by a person in the face of disconfirming evidence. Represents how we resist change once a schema has been established.

Causal attribution is the way in which we offer explanations, reasons, or causes for either our own or other people's social behaviour. Causes are classified into two main categories: internal or dispositional and external or situational.

Causal schemata model is applied when only a single instance of behaviour is known about. In making attributions to single events the attributor relies on his or her knowledge and experience, i.e. schemata, of causes of behaviour.

Central trait is a personality trait, suggested by Asch (1946), which has a strong influence on the impression formed of another person and which also influences other traits we assume another person to possess. The most common central trait is the warm–cold dimension.

Circumstance attribution is where a causal explanation is given based on a unique set of circumstances. Technically it is when distinctiveness is high, and consistency and consensus low. See covariation model.

Cognitive miser represents the idea that people have limited capacity to process information, may be unwilling to expend mental effort, and trade off accuracy for speed in making social judgements.

Collectivist cultures are where interdependence and the general welfare of the culture or country are emphasised, e.g. Chinese culture. Such cultures tend to emphasise situational or external attributions. See individualistic cultures.

Consensus information is to do with how other people behave in similar situations. If most people behave in the same way, consensus is high, if differently, consensus is low. See covariation model.

Consistency information is whether the person behaves in the same or different ways in a range of social situations. High consistency is where behaviour is similar across social situations, and low where different. See covariation model.

Contact hypothesis is the idea that contact between groups, especially majority and minority groups, will reduce prejudice and discrimination. To be most effective groups should have similar status, interact and work co-operatively on a task.

Controllability refers to whether the person feels that he or she has personal control over their behaviour, where a person does not it is uncontrollable. See Weiner's model.

Co-operative learning groups are groups of school children or students that must share what each individual in the group has information about in order to learn or understand the task fully. The jigsaw method depends upon the use of co-operative learning groups.

Correspondent inference theory is concerned with how we make internal or dispositional attributions to explain another person's behaviour. Of importance are non-common effects and hedonic relevance.

Covariation model is a general model of attribution proposed by Kelley. The model uses distinctiveness, consistency and consensus information to determine whether an internal, external, or circumstance attribution is appropriate.

Deliberative attributions result from a person thinking more deeply about a person's behaviour and the social context in which it takes place before making a causal attribution. See deliberative thought.

Deliberative thought is where a person takes time and makes a conscious mental effort to think things through more deeply before making a social judgement. By contrast see spontaneous thought.

Discounting principle is when unlikely causes of behaviour are discounted in favour of the one thought to be most likely. Used when you do not have information about a person's past behaviour. See augmenting principle.

Discrimination is where a person behaves negatively or positively towards a member of a social group or the social group as a whole. Discrimination often results in intergroup conflict because it is unfair and unjustified. See also prejudice.

Dispositional attributions are causes of behaviour to do with a person's personality traits, temperament, etc. Also characterised as internal causes.

Distinctiveness information concerns whether or not a person's behaviour is specific to that social situation or whether the behaviour occurs across a range of social situations. In the former case distinctiveness is high, in the latter, low. See covariation model.

Ecological validity refers to how well a laboratory experiment in social psychology reflects or can be related to everyday, real life. Experiments with high ecological validity can be readily generalised to our social lives; those with low ecological validity cannot be generalised. Experiments low in ecological validity may be of limited value in social psychology.

Egoistic deprivation is where an individual feels relative deprivation in comparison to another individual or group of individuals belonging to the same social group as themselves. See also relative deprivation theory.

Ethnocentric bias. See group-serving bias.

Event schemas are mental representations of what we normally expect to happen in a frequently experienced social situation. For example, going to the cinema or eating out in a restaurant. See also scripts and social schemas.

External causes are those which explain behaviour by reference to factors and pressures to do with the social situation. Such causes are external to the person and may be difficult to control. See also internal causes.

False consensus effect is the tendency for people to overestimate how common their own behaviour is amongst other people. This extends to thinking that attitudes held by a person are more widely held in other people generally.

Fraternalist deprivation is where an individual or social group to which the individual belongs feels deprived relative to another social group. See also relative deprivation theory.

Frustration and aggression is an explanation of prejudice and discrimination based on the idea that aggression results from frustration and the aggression is often displaced on to vulnerable, lower status, minority groups.

Fundamental attribution error is the tendency to overestimate the importance of dispositions and underestimate the importance of situational factors when making attributions about another person's behaviour.

Gestalt psychology is an approach which regards the 'whole as greater than the sum of the parts'; this is in contrast, for example, to a behaviourist approach which assumes that all behaviour can be broken down into constituent components.

Group-serving attributional bias is where members of a ingroup make internal attributions to positive behaviour by members of the ingroup and situational attributions to negative behaviour by outgroup members.

Hedonic relevance is behaviour which has a positive or negative effect on the person who is making the attribution; in effect the behaviour is personally of relevance to the attributor. See correspondence inference theory.

Heuristics of thinking are mental shortcuts that people use to make judgements or social inferences. The most commonly used are availability, anchoring and adjustment and representativeness. See also cognitive miser.

Implicit personality theory is a general expectation held by people about the characteristics and attitude of a person based on knowledge about central traits. See also impression formation.

Impression formation in social psychology is concerned with understanding how we form impressions of another person's personality traits, attitudes, beliefs, etc. See also first impressions, primacy effects, and recency effects.

Impression management is where you attempt to present and manage a favourable impression of yourself to other people. This may be done through either or both self-enhancement and other-enhancement. See also impression formation.

Individualistic cultures are those where personality, independence and individual perspectives are emphasised; such cultures tend to emphasise trait or internal attributions. See also collectivist culture.

Intergroup conflict is conflict or aggressive behaviour which takes place between social groups. See also social identity theory and realistic group conflict.

Internal causes are those which explain behaviour through reference to something about the person, such as personality traits, temperament, mood, or dispositions. See also external causes.

Jigsaw method is a procedure used in school classrooms to enhance interaction or contact between children of different ethnic or racial groups. See also co-operative learning groups.

Linguistic ingroup bias is where ingroup members talk about outgroup members in abstract terms, whereas when talking about other ingroup members more concrete and specific language is used.

Locus of control is a personality factor proposed by Rotter to explain individual differences in attributions. Internal locus of control is where people see themselves able to influence the outcome; external locus of control is behaviour beyond their control.

Locus refers to whether the cause is to do with the person (internal) or to do with situational factors (external). See Weiner's model.

Minimal group paradigm is an experimental procedure used by Tajfel to investigate intergroup discrimination in the absence of any obvious competition between groups. Participants are given a matrix and asked to allocate points to the ingroup and outgroup.

Findings show that ingroup members show favouritism to their own group.

Mortality salience hypothesis states that when people are reminded of their own mortality they will seek increased protection for and provide enhanced support for their own culture, beliefs, religion, etc. See also terror management theory.

New racism is a more subtle type of racism evidenced by denial that discrimination takes place, irritation at minorities asking for equal treatment and resentment that disadvantaged groups get special treatment. See also racism.

Non-common effects are consequences or outcomes of behaviour which are unexpected or specific only to that behaviour or person. See correspondence inference theory.

Non-voluntary behaviour is behaviour which a person has not planned in advance or may not have control over. For example, an extrovert will normally behave in extrovert ways and not be able to be introverted if asked. See also voluntary behaviour.

Normative theories prescribe what should normally or generally be the case. Normative theories may not reflect the attributions people actually make in their everyday lives.

Objectification is a process to do with social representations whereby complex or abstract ideas are translated into specific concrete images, so making them easier to understand.

Outgroup homogeneity is the tendency to perceive outgroup members as all the same or homogeneous, and ingroup members as having individual differences. Related to self-categorisation theory and stereotypes.

Peripheral trait is a personality trait, suggested by Asch (1946), which has only a minor influence on the impression formed of another person. See also central trait.

Person schemas are mental representations which summarise what you know about a person, or a role that a person fulfils; for example, 'your best friend' person schema. See also prototypes and social schemas.

Prejudice is an unjustified attitude, which may be negative or positive, towards an individual based on that individual's membership of a social group. See also discrimination.

Primacy effect is where information we are provided with first about a person has the most influence on the impression that is formed of the person. Initial impressions are often long-lasting. See recency effects.

Prototype is a special type of person schema representing ideal types, for example, your ideal best friend, or your ideal romantic partner. See also social schemas.

Racism is where people hold unjustified prejudicial attitudes to people of another racial grouping. Most commonly researched in relation to White and Black people. See also new racism.

Realistic group conflict was investigated by Sherif in the famous 'Robber's cave experiment'. The basic idea is that prejudice and discrimination between groups arises from direct competition for valued resources. Shared goals of two or more groups, where only one group can obtain the goal at the expense of another, will result in competition and be followed by intergroup conflict.

Recency effect is where information presented last or later has a greater influence on the impression we form of a person. Recency effects are most likely to occur when there is a time delay between initial and later information. See also primacy effect.

Relative deprivation theory states that people act negatively towards other social groups when they perceive themselves and their own social group as not enjoying a standard of living they believe they deserve. The larger the difference between actual attainments and expectations, the greater the degree of social discontent felt by the person or social group.

Representativeness heuristic is used to make judgements of similarity, employing both experience and social schemas, particularly prototypes. See also heuristics of thinking.

Right wing authoritarian scale is a revised and modern version of the F-scale but measuring only authoritarian aggression, authoritarian submission and conventionalism. This questionnaire does not suffer from an acquiescent response set as does the F-scale.

Role schemas are mental representations of the typical behaviours you expect of a person who occupies a social role. For example, leadership schema or doctor schema. See also social schemas.

Scapegoat is where an individual uses a weak or vulnerable group to enact prejudice and discrimination on, and where the group is unfairly treated because of this.

Schematic traits are traits that are of central importance to a person. Related to central traits, opposite to aschematic traits.

Scripts. See event schemas.

Self-categorisation theory states that social identity is based on self-categorisation, hence ingroup favouritism can only be seen where you regard yourself as belonging to that social group in the first place. This has the advantage over Social Identity Theory since social categorisation theory incorporates how a person categorises him- or herself according to a social group.

Self-effacement bias, also known as the modesty bias. Evident in collectivistic cultures where success is attributed more to external factors and failure to personal characteristics. The opposite to self-serving bias found in Western, individualistic cultures.

Self-enhancing bias is where we attribute causes for our own behaviour that put us in a more favourable light. See also self-protective and self-serving bias.

Self-esteem is the general evaluation, good or bad, that we make of ourselves in relation to ability, sociability, etc. High self-esteem gives us confidence, low self-esteem is negative.

Self-fulfilling prophecy is where expectations we hold about ourselves or other people cause or influence the person to behave in ways consistent with the expectations. Initial expectations may be wrong, but conforming to expectations results in them becoming realised and hence a self-fulfilling prophecy.

Self-protective bias is where attributions for failure or poor performance are made in such a way as to protect the person. This usually results in external or situational attributions being made. See self-serving bias.

Self-schemas are cognitive representations about yourself which are generalisations based on past experience and how you believe yourself to be. See also social schemas.

Self-serving bias is where people tend to take credit for their successes and deny responsibility for failure. In the former, positive internal attributions are made; in the latter, external or situational attributions.

Sexism is unjustified prejudice and discrimination toward members of the opposite sex. Most commonly researched in terms of male sexist attitudes to women, but can also be the other way round.

Situational causes are causes external to the person and concern such factors as social pressure, social norms, social rules, etc. See also external causes.

Social cognition concerns the ways in which we interpret, analyse and remember information about ourselves and other people in different social contexts.

Social identity theory states that people understand and evaluate their individual identities through being members of a social group. The ingroup member makes evaluative comparisons with outgroups. In making ingroup–outgroup comparisons people seek to maintain a high level of self-esteem.

Social perception is the process through which we seek to know and understand other people; the term is often used interchangeably with social cognition.

Social representations are the mental representations we make about the culture and sub-cultures in which we live. They come from interaction with other people. Social representations may be of a culture, a tradition or a fashion. The former is most resistant to change and the latter changes more rapidly.

Social schemas are cognitive structures which represent knowledge about people and their attributes and relationships between attributes. See person, self and event schemas.

Spontaneous attributions are causal attributions that a person makes without engaging in much or any thought. See spontaneous thought.

Spontaneous thought is where attitudes, judgements and attributions come to mind automatically and without the person making much mental effort. See deliberative thought as a contrast.

Stability refers to whether an internal or external cause of behaviour is stable and enduring or unstable and temporary. See Weiner's model.

Stereotype is a belief that people identified as belonging to a particular social grouping all share the same attitudes, personality characteristics, etc. Stereotypes ignore differences between people. May result in sexism or racism.

Superordinate goals were used by Sherif to reduce realistic group conflict. Superordinate goals can only be achieved by both groups working together and co-operating to achieve a goal. Reduce intergroup conflict when a number of different tasks are worked at co-operatively by two groups.

Terror management theory explains prejudice and intolerance through a basic instinct for self-preservation which is threatened by the knowledge that we are mortal and will die. Cultures provide security and meaning for a person; hence other cultures, religions, etc. threaten one's own culture.

Voluntary behaviour is behaviour which is under a person's control and usually the result of planning and prior intentions. The opposite is non-voluntary or involuntary behaviour.

Weiner's achievement attribution model was formulated to explain success and failure at academic achievement. Uses the three dimensions of locus, stability, and controllability to arrive at an internal or external attribution.

Bibliography

Abrams, D. and Hogg, M. A. (eds) (1998) *Social Identity and Social Cognition*, Oxford: Blackwell.

Adorno, T. W., Frenkel-Brunswick, E., Levinson, D. T. and Sanford, R. N. (1950) *The Authoritarian Personality*, 43, 709–26.

Alloy, L. B. and Tabachnik, N. (1984) Assessment of covariation by humans and animals: the joint influence of prior expectations and current situational information, *Psychological Review*, 91, 112–49.

Altmeyer, B. (1981) *Right-wing authoritarianism*, Winnipeg: University of Manitoba Press.

—— (1996) *The authoritarian spectre*, Cambridge, MA: Harvard University Press.

—— (1998) The Other 'Authoritarian Personality'. In M. P. Zanna (ed.), *Advances in Experimental Social Psychology*, vol. 30, San Diego: Academic Press.

Anderson, S. M. and Klatzky, R. L. (1987) Traits and stereotypes: levels of categorisation in person perception, *Journal of Personality and Social Psychology*, 53, 235–46.

Archer, D., Iritani, B., Kimes, D. and Barios, M. (1983) Five studies of sex difference in facial prominence, *Journal of Personality and Social Psychology*, 45, 725–35.

Aronson, E. (1999) *The Social Animal*, 8th edn, New York: Worth Publishers.

Aronson, E., Stephan, W., Sikes, J., Blaney, N. and Snapp, M. (1978) *Co-operation in the Classroom*, Beverley Hills, CA: Sage.

Asch, S. E. (1946) Forming impressions of personality, *Journal of Abnormal and Social Psychology*, 41, 258–90.

Augostinos, M. and Walker, I. (1995) *Social Cognition: An Integrated Approach*, London, Sage Publications.

Baron, R. A. and Byrne, D. (1997) *Social Psychology*, 8th edn, Boston, MA: Allyn and Bacon.

—— (2000) *Social Psychology*, 9th edn, Boston: Allyn and Bacon.

Bartlett, F. A. (1932) *A Study in Experimental and Social Psychology*, New York: Cambridge University Press.

Baumeister, R. F. and Leary, M. R. (1995) The need to belong: desire for interpersonal attachments as a fundamental human motivation, *Psychological Bulletin*, 117, 491–529.

Baxter, T. L. and Goldberg, L. R. (1988) Perceived behavioural inconsistency underlying trait attributions to oneself and another: an extension of the actor–observer effect, *Personality and Social Psychology Bulletin*, 13, 437–47.

Beauvois, J-L. (1984) *La psychologie quotidienne*, Paris: Presses Universitaires de France.

Berkowitz, L. (1962) *Aggression: A Social Psychological Analysis*, New York: McGraw-Hill.

Biddle, S. J. H. and Hill, A. B. (1992) Relationships between attributions and emotions in a laboratory-based sporting contest, *Journal of Sports Sciences*, 10, 65–75.

Binning, J. F. , Goldstein, M. A., Garcia, M. F. and Scatteregia, J. H. (1988) Effects of pre-interview impressions on questioning strategies in same- and opposite-sex employment interviews, *Journal of Applied Psychology*, 73, 30–7.

Blanchard, P. A., Weigel, R. H. and Cook, S. W. (1975) The effect of relative competence of group members upon interpersonal attraction in co-operating inter-racial groups, *Journal of Personality and Social Psychology*, 19, 303–11.

Bobo, L. (1988) Attitudes towards the black political movement: trends, measuring and effects on racial policy preferences, *Social Psychology Quarterly*, 51, 287–302.

Breakwell, G. M. (1978) Some effects of marginal social identity. In H. Tajfel (ed.), *Differentiation Between Social Groups*, London: Academic Press.

Brewin, C. R. (1984) Perceived controllability of life-events and willingness to prescribe psychotropic drugs, *British Journal of Social Psychology*, 23, 285–7.

Brown, R. (1978) Divided we fall: an analysis of relations between sections of a factory workforce. In H. Tajfel (ed.), *Differentiation between Social Groups: Studies in the Social Psychology of Intergroup Relations*, London: Academic Press.

—— (1995) *Prejudice: Its Social Psychology*, Oxford: Blackwell.

Brown, R. and Smith, A. (1989) Perceptions of and by minority groups: the case of women in academia, *European Journal of Social Psychology*, 19, 61 75.

Bruner, J. and Taguiri, R. (1954) Person Perception. In G. Lindzey (ed.), *Handbook of Social Psychology*, vol. 2, Reading, MA: Addison Wesley.

Bull, R. and Rumsey, N. (1988) *The Social Psychology of Facial Appearance*, New York: Springer-Verlag.

Burger, J. M. (1981) Motivational biases in the attribution of responsibility for an accident: a meta-analysis of the defensive-attribution hypothesis, *Psychological Bulletin*, 90, 496–512.

Campbell, D. T. (1967) Stereotypes and the perception of group differences, *American Psychologist*, 22, 817–29.

Cheu, H., Yates, B. T. and McGinnies, E. (1988) Effects of involvement on observers' estimates of consensus, distinctiveness and consistency, *Personality and Social Psychology Bulletin*, 14, 468 78.

Chrisler, J. C. and Levy, K. B. (1990) The media construct a menstrual monster: a content analysis of MPS articles in the popular press, *Women and Health*, 16, 89–104.

Christie, R. (1954) Authoritarianism re-examined. In R. Christie and M. Jahoda (eds), *Studies in the Scope and Method of the Authoritarian Personality*, Glencoe, IL: Free Press.

Christie, R. and Cook, P. (1958) A guide to published literature relating to the Authoritarian Personality through 1956, *Journal of Psychology*, 45, 191–9.

Cohen, C. E. (1981) Person categories and social perception: testing some boundaries of the processing effects of prior knowledge, *Journal of Personality and Social Psychology*, 40, 441–52.

Cohen, E. G. (1984) The desegregated school: problems in status, power and interethnic climate. In N. Miller and M. B. Brewer (eds), *Groups in Contact: The Psychology of Desegregation*, Orlando, FL: Academic Press.

Corsaro, W. A. (1990) The underlife of the nursery school: young children's social representations of adult rules. In G. Dureen and

B. Lloyd (eds), *Social Representations and the Development of Knowledge*, Cambridge: Cambridge University Press.

Cox, R. H. (1998) *Sport Psychology: Concepts and Applications*, 4th edn, Boston, MA: McGraw-Hill.

Darley, J. M. and Fazio, R. H. (1980) Expectancy confirmation processes arising in the social interaction sequence, *American Psychologist*, 35, 867–81.

Darley, J. M. and Gross, P. H. (1983) A hypothesis-continuing bias in labelling effects, *Journal of Personality and Social Psychology*, 44, 20–33.

Dawes, R. (1989) Statistical criteria for establishing a truly false consensus effect, *Journal of Experimental Social Psychology*, 25, 1–17.

de Rosa, A. S. (1987) The social representation of mental illness in children and adults. In W. Doise and S. Moscovici (eds), *Current Issues in European Social Psychology*, vol. 2, Cambridge: Cambridge University Press.

Diab, L. N. (1970) A study of intragroup and intergroup relations among experimentally produced small groups, *Genetic Psychology Monographs*, 82, 49–82.

Dix, T., Ruble, D. N., Grusec, J. E. and Nixon, S. (1986) Social cognition in parents: inferential and affective reactions to children of three age levels, *Child Development*, 57, 879–94.

Dollard, J., Doob, L. N., Miller, M. E., Mowrer, D. K. and Sears, R. R. (1939) *Frustration and Aggression*, New Haven, CT: Yale University Press.

Dovidio, J. F. and Fazio, R. H. (1992) New technologies for the direct and indirect assessment of attitudes. In J. M. Taylor (ed.), *Questions about Questions: Inquiries into the Cognitive Bases of Surveys*, New York: Russell Sage.

Dovidio, J. F. and Gaertner, S. L. (1993) Stereotypes and evaluative intergroup bias. In D. M. Mackie and D. L. Hamilton (eds), *Affect, Cognition and Stereotyping: Interactive Processes in Group Perception*, San Diego, CA: Academic Press.

Ellemers, N., Wilke, H. and Van Knippenberg, A. (1993) Effects of the legitimacy of low group or individual status as individual and collective status-enhancement strategies, *Journal of Personality and Social Psychology*, 64, 766–78.

Eysenck, H.J. (1973) *The Inequality of Man*, London: Temple Smith.

Fazio, R.H. (1990) Multiple processes by which attitudes guide behaviour: the MODE model as an integrative framework. In M.P. Zanna (ed.), *Advances in Experimental Social Psychology*, vol. 23, New York: Academic Press.

Feingold, A. (1992) Good looking people are not what we think, *Psychological Bulletin*, 111, 304–41.

Feldman, R. S. (1998) *Social Psychology*, 2nd edn, Englewood Cliffs, NJ: Prentice Hall.

Festinger, L. (1975) *A Theory of Cognitive Dissonance*, Palo Alto, CA: Stanford University Press.

Fiske, S. (1995) Social Cognition. In A. Tesser (ed.), *Advanced Social Psychology*, New York: McGraw-Hill.

Fiske, S.T. and Neuberg, S. L. (1990) A continuum of impression formation, from category-based to individuating processes: influences of information on attention and interpretation. In M. P. Zanna (ed.), *Advances in Experimental Social Psychology*, vol. 2.3, New York: Academic Press.

Fiske, S. T. and Taylor, S. E. (1991) *Social Cognition*, 2nd edn, New York: McGraw-Hill.

Fletcher, G. J. O. and Ward, C. (1988) Attribution theory and processes: a cross-cultural perspective. In M. H. Bond (ed.), *The Cross-Cultural Challenge to Social Psychology*, Newbury Park, CA: Sage Publications.

Fry, P. S. and Ghosh, R. (1980) Attributions of success and failure: comparison of cultural differences between Asian and Caucasian children, *Journal of Cross-Cultural Psychology*, 11, 343–63.

Frye, D. (1991) The origins of intention in infancy. In D. Frye and C. Moore (eds), *Children's Theories of Mind: Mental States and Social Understandings*, Hillside, NJ: Erlbaum.

Furnham, A. (1982) The perception of poverty amongst adolescents, *Journal of Adolescence*, 5, 135–47.

Gaertner, S. L. and Dovidio, J. F. (1986) The aversive form of racism. In J. F. Dovidio and S. L. Gaertner (eds), *Prejudice, Discrimination and Racism*, New York: Academic Press.

Gaertner, S. L., Mann, J., Dovidio, J. F., Murrell, A. J. and Pomare, M. (1990) How does co-operation reduce intergroup bias? *Journal of Personality and Social Psychology*, 59, 692–704.

Gaertner, S. L., Mann, J., Murrell, A. and Dovidio, J. F. (1989) Reducing intergroup bias: the benefits of recategorisation, *Journal of Personality and Social Psychology*, 57, 239–49.

Garland, H., Hardy, A. and Stephenson, L. (1975) Information search as affected by attribution type and response category, *Personality and Social Psychology Bulletin*, 1, 612–15.

Gerard, H. B. and Hoyt, M. F. (1974) Distinctiveness of social categorisation and attitude toward ingroup members, *Journal of Personality and Social Psychology*, 29, 836–42.

Gerrig, R. J. and Prentice, D. A. (1991) The representation of fictional information, *Psychological Science*, 2, 336–40.

Gilbert, D. T. (1989) Thinking lightly about others: automatic components of the social inference process. In J. S. Uleman and J. A. Bargh (eds), *Unintended Thought: Causes and Consequences for Judgement, Emotion and Behaviour*, New York: Guildford.

Gilbert, D. T. and Malone, P. S. (1995) The correspondence bias, *Psychological Bulletin*, 117, 21–8.

Gilbert, D. T., Pelham, B. W. and Krull, D. S. (1988) Of thoughts unspoken: social inference and the self-regulation of behaviour, *Journal of Personality and Social Psychology*, 55, 685–94.

Gilbert, D. T., Pelham, B. W. and Krull, D. S. (1988) On cognitive busyness: when person perceivers meet persons perceived, *Journal of Personality and Social Psychology*, 54, 733–9.

Greenberg, J., Pyszczynski, T., Solomon, S., Rosenblatt, A., Veeder, M., Kirkland, S. and Lynn, D. (1990) Evidence for terror management theory II: the effects of mortality salience to those who threaten or bolster a cultural world view, *Journal of Personality and Social Psychology*, 58, 308–18.

Greenberg, J., Solomon, S. and Pyszczynski, T. (1997) Terror management theory of self-esteem and cultural world views: empirical assessments and cultural refinements. In M. P. Zanna (ed.), *Advances in Experimental Social Psychology*, vol. 29, San Diego, CA: Academic Press.

Greenberg, J., Williams, K. D. and O'Brien, M. K. (1986) Considering the harshest verdict first: biasing effects on mock jurors verdicts, *Personality and Social Psychology Bulletin*, 12, 41–50.

Gurr, T. R. (1970) *Why men rebel*, Princetown, NJ: Princetown University Press.

Hamilton, D. C. and Mackie, D. M. (1993) Cognitive and affective processes in intergroup perception: the developing interface. In D. Mackie and D. Hamilton (eds), *Affect, Cognition and Stereotyping: Interactive Processes in Intergroup Perception*, San Diego, CA: Academic Press.

Harmon-Jones, E., Greenberg, J., Solomon, S. and Simon, L. (1996) The effects of mortality salience on intergroup bias between minimal groups, *European Journal of Social Psychology*, 25, 781–5.

Heath, L., Acklin, M. and Wiley, K. (1991) Cognitive heuristics and AIDS risk assessment among physicians, *Journal of Applied Social Psychology*, 21, 1859–67.

Heider, F. (1958) *The Psychology of Interpersonal Relations*, New York: Wiley.

Henderson, J. (1999) *Memory and Forgetting*, London: Routledge.

Hendy, H. M. and Boyer, B. J. (1993) Gender differences in attributions for triathlon performance, *Sex Roles*, 29, 527–43.

Herzlich, C. (1973) *Health and Illness: A Social Psychological Analysis*, London: Academic Press.

Hewstone, M. (1989) *Causal Attribution: From Cognitive Processes to Cognitive Beliefs*, Oxford: Blackwell.

Hewstone, M. R. C. and Brown, R. J. (1986) Contact is not enough: an intergroup perspective on the contact hypothesis. In M. R. C. Hewstone and R. J. Brown (eds), *Contact and Conflict in Intergroup Encounters*, Oxford: Blackwell.

Hewstone, M., Fincham, F. and Jaspers, J. (1981) Social categorisation and similarity in intergroup behaviour: a replication with penalties, *European Journal of Social Psychology*, 11, 101–7.

Hilton, D. J. and Slugoski, B. R. (1986) Knowledge-based causal attributions: the abnormal conditions focus model, *Psychological Review*, 93, 75–88.

Hogg, M. A. and Hardie, E. A. (1991) Social attraction, personal attraction and self-categorisation: a field study, *Personality and Social Psychology Bulletin*, 17, 175–80.

Hogg, M. A., Turner, J. C., Nascimento-Schulze, C. and Spriggs, D. (1986) Social categorisation, intergroup behaviour and self-esteem: two experiments, *Revista de Psicología Social*, 1, 23–37.

Holder, E. E. and Levi, D. J. (1988) Mental health and locus of control: SCL-90-R and Levenson's IPC scales, *Journal of Clinical Psychology*, 44, 753–5.

Hovland, C. and Sears, R. R. (1940) Minor studies in aggression IV: Correlation Lynchings with economic indices, *Journal of Psychology*, 9, 301–10.

Hyman, M. M. and Sheatsley, P. B. (1954) The Authoritarian Personality: a methodological critique. In R. Christie and M. Jahoda (eds), *Studies in the Scope and Method of the Authoritarian Personality, Glencoe*, IL: Free Press.

Jodelet, D. (1991) *Madness and Social Representations*, Hemel Hempstead: Harvester Wheatsheaf.

Johnson, J. T. (1986) The knowledge of what might have been: affective and attributional consequences of near outcomes, *Personality and Social Psychology Bulletin*, 12, 51–62.

Johnson, T. J., Feigenbaum, R. and Weisbeg, M. (1964) Some determinants and consequences of the teacher's perception of causality, *Journal of Educational Psychology*, 55, 237–46.

Jones, E. E. and Davis, K. E. (1965) From acts to dispositions: the attribution process in person perception. In L. Berkowitz (ed.), *Advances in Experimental Social Psychology* (vol. 2), New York: Academic Press.

Jones, E. E. and Nisbett, R. E. (1972) The actor and the observer: divergent perceptions of the causes of behaviour. In E. E. Jones, D. E. Kanouse, H. H. Kelley, R. E. Nisbett, S. Valins and B. Weiner (eds), *Attribution: Perceiving the Causes of Behaviour*, Morristown, NJ: General Learning Press.

Jones, J. M. (1986) Racism: a cultural analysis of the problem. In J. F. Dovidio and S. L. Gaertner (eds), *Prejudice, Discrimination and Racism*, Orlando, FL: Academic Press.

Kashima, Y. and Triandis, H. C. (1986) The self-serving bias in attributions as a coping strategy: a cross-cultural study, *Journal of Cross-Cultural Psychology*, 17, 83–97.

Kassin, S. M. and Ellis, S. A. (1988) On the acquisition of the discounting principle: an experimental test of a social-developmental model, *Child Development*, 59, 950–60.

Kassin, S. M. and Pryor, J. B. (1985) The development of attribution processes. In J. B. Pryor and J. D. Day (eds), *The Development of Social Cognition*, New York: Springer-Verlag.

Kelley, H. H. (1950) The warm–cold variable in first impressions of persons, *Journal of Personality*, 18, 431–9.

—— (1967) Attribution theory in social psychology. In D. Levine (ed.), *Nebraska Symposium on Motivation* (vol. 15), Lincoln: University of Nebraska Press.

—— (1972) Causal schemata and the attribution process. In E. E. Jones, H. H. Kelley, R. E. Nesbitt, S. Valins and B. Weiner (eds), *Attribution: Perceiving the Causes of Behaviour*, Morristown, NJ: General Learning Press.

Kenny, D. A. (1991) A general model of consensus and accuracy in interpersonal perception, *Psychological Review*, 98, 155–63.

Klandermans, B. (1984) Mobilisation and participation: social psychological expansions of resource mobilisation theory, *American Sociological Review*, 49, 583–600.

Klein, J. G. (1991) Negativity effects in impression formation: a test in the political arena, *Personality and Social Psychology Bulletin*, 17, 412–18.

Kruglanski, A. W. (1975) The endogenous–exogenous partition in attribution theory, *Psychological Review*, 82, 387–406.

—— (1977) The place of naïve contents in a theory of attribution: reflections on Calder's and Zuckerman's critique of the endogenous–exogenous partition, *Personality and Social Psychology*, 3, 592–605.

Kruglanski, A. W. and Freund, T. (1983) The freezing and unfreezing of lay inferences: effects on impressional primacy, ethnic stereotyping and numerical anchoring, *Journal of Experimental Social Psychology*, 19, 448–68.

Krull, D. S. and Erickson, D. J. (1995) Inferential hopscotch: how people draw social inferences from behaviour, *Current Directions in Psychological Science*, 4, 35–8.

Kunda, Z. and Oleson, K. C. (1995) Maintaining stereotypes in the face of disconfirmation: constructing grounds for subtyping deviants, *Journal of Personality and Social Psychology*, 68, 565–79.

Langer, E. J., Bashner, R. S. and Chanowitz, B. (1985) Decreasing prejudice by increasing discrimination, *Journal of Personality and Social Psychology*, 49, 113–20.

Lefcourt, H. M. (1982) *Locus of Control: Current Trends in Theory and Research*, 2nd edn, Hillsdale, NJ: Erlbaum.

Levesque, M. J. and Kenny, D. A. (1993) Accuracy of behavioural predictions at zero acquaintance: a social relations analysis, *Journal of Personality and Social Psychology*, 65, 1178–87.

Lord, C. G. (1997) *Social Psychology*, Fort Worth: Harcourt Bruce College Publishers.

Luchins, A. S. (1957) Primacy-recency in impression formation. In C. Hovland (ed.), *The Order of Presentation in Persuasion*, New Haven, CT: Yale University Press.

Maas, A. and Acuri, L. (1996) Language and stereotyping. In C.N. Macrae, C. Stangor and M. Hewstone (eds), *Stereotypes and Stereotyping*, New York: Guildford.

Maas, A., Salvi, D., Arcuri, L. and Semin, G. (1989) Language use in intergroup contexts: the linguistic intergroup bias, *Journal of Personality and Social Psychology*, 57, 981–93.

Macleod, C. and Campbell, L. (1992) Memory accessibility and probability judgements: an experimental evaluation, *Journal of Personality and Social Psychology*, 63, 890–902.

MaCrae, C. N., Bodenhausen, G. V., Milne, A. B. and Jelton, J. (1994) Out of mind but back in sight: stereotypes on the rebound, *Journal of Personality and Social Psychology*, 67, 808–17.

Marks, G. and Miller, N. (1987) Ten years of research on the false consensus effect: an empirical and theoretical review, *Psychological Bulletin*, 102, 72–90.

Markus, H. (1977) Self-schemata and processing information about the self, *Journal of Personality and Social Psychology*, 35, 63–78.

Markus, H. and Nurius, P. (1986) Possible selves, *American Psychologist*, 51, 858–66.

McArthur, L. Z. (1972) The how and what of why: some determinants and consequences of causal attribution, *Journal of Personality and Social Psychology*, 22, 171–93.

McAuley, E., Russell, D. and Gross, J. B. (1983) Affective consequences of winning and losing: an attributional analysis, *Journal of Sport Psychology*, 5, 278–87.

McAuley, E., Duncan, T. E. and Russell, D. (1992) Measuring causal attributions: the revised causal dimension scale, *Personality and Social Psychology Bulletin*, 18, 566–73.

McKelvie, S. J. (1990) The Asch primacy effect: robust but not infallible, *Journal of Social Behaviour and Personality*, 5, 135–50.

Miller, J. G. (1984) Culture and the development of everyday social explanation, *Journal of Personality and Social Psychology*, 46, 961–78.

Miller, N. and Davidson-Podgorny, F. (1987) Theoretical models of intergroup relations and the use of co-operative teams as an intervention for desegregated settings. In C. Hendrick (ed.), *Group Processes and Intergroup Relations: Review of Personality and Social Psychology*, vol. 9, Beverley Hills, CA: Sage.

Miller, P. H. and Aloise, P. A. (1989) Young children's understanding of the psychological causes of behaviour: a review, *Child Development*, 60, 257–85.

Miller, R. S. and Schlenker, B. R. (1985) Egotism in group members:

public and private attributions of responsibility for group performance, *Social Psychology Quarterly*, 48, 85–9.

Mooney, S. P., Sherman, M. F. and LoPresto, C. T. (1991) Academic locus of control, self-esteem, and perceived distance from home as predictors of college adjustment, *Journal of Counselling and Development*, 69, 445–8.

Morris, M. W. and Peng, K. (1994) Culture and cause: American and Chinese attributions for social and physical events, *Journal of Personality and Social Psychology*, 67, 949–71.

Moscovici, S. (1972) Society and theory in social psychology. In J. Israel and H. Tajfel (eds), *The Context of Social Psychology: A Critical Assessment*, London: Academic Press.

—— (1981) On social representations. In J. P. Fargas (ed.), *Social Cognition: Perspectives on Everyday Understanding*, London: Academic Press.

—— (1984) The phenomenon of social representations. In R. M. Farr and S. Moscovici (eds), *Social Representations*, Cambridge: Cambridge University Press.

Moscovici, S. and Hewstone, M. (1983) Social representations and social explanations: from the 'naïve' to the 'amateur' scientist. In M. Hewstone (ed.), *Attribution Theory: Social and Functional Extensions*, Oxford: Blackwell.

Murray, M. and McMillan, C. (1989) Age differences in perception of cancer. Paper presented at Annual Conference of Northern Ireland branch of British Psychological Society, Virginia, Co. Cavan.

Myers, D.G. (1996) *Social Psychology*, New York: McGraw-Hill.

—— (1998) *Social Psychology*, 5th edn, New York: McGraw-Hill.

Nesdale, A. R. and Pope, S. (1985) Young children's causal attributions and performance expectations on skilled tasks, *British Journal of Developmental Psychology*, 3, 183–90.

Newman, L. S. (1993) How individualists interpret behaviour: idiocentrism and spontaneous trait inference, *Social Cognition*, 11, 243–69.

Nisbett, R. E., Caputo, C., Legant, P. and Maracek, J. (1973) Behaviour as seen by the actor and the observer, *Journal of Personality and Social Psychology*, 27, 154–64.

Nisbett, R. E. and Ross, L. (1980) *Human Inference: Strategies and*

Shortcomings of Social Judgement, Englewood Cliffs, NJ: Prentice Hall.

Park, B. (1986) A method for studying the development of impressions of real people, *Journal of Personality and Social Psychology*, 51, 907–17.

Pennington, D. C., Gillen, K. and Hill, P. (1999) *Social Psychology*, London: Arnold.

Phares, E. J. (1976) *Locus of Control in Personality*, Morristown, NJ: General Learning Press.

Platz, S. J. and Hosch, H. M. (1988) Cross-racial/ethnic eye-witness identification: a field study, *Journal of Applied Social Psychology*, 18, 972–84.

Plous, S. (1989) Thinking the unthinkable: the effects of anchoring on likelihood estimates of nuclear war, *Journal of Applied Social Psychology*, 19, 67–91.

Potter, J. and Wetherell, M. (1987) *Discourse and Social Psychology: Beyond Attitudes and Behaviour*, London: Sage.

Rokeach, M. (ed.) (1960) *The Open and Closed Mind*, New York: Basic Books.

Rookes, P. and Willson, J. (1999) *Perception: Theory, Development and Organisation*, London: Routledge.

Rosenthal, R. (1985) From unconscious experimenter bias to teacher expectancy effects. In J.B. Dusek, V.C. Hall and W.J. Meyer (eds), *Teacher Expectancies*, Hillsdale, NJ: Erlbaum.

Rosenthal, R. and Jacobson, L. F. (1968) *Pygmalion in the Classroom*, New York: Holt, Rinehart & Winston.

Ross, L. (1977) The intuitive psychologist and his shortcomings. In L. Berkowitz (ed.), *Advances in Experimental Social Psychology*, vol. 10, New York: Academic Press.

Ross, L., Amabile, T. M. and Steinmetz, J. L. (1997) Social roles, social control and biases in social perception processes, *Journal of Personality and Social Psychology*, 35, 485–94.

Ross, L., Greene, D. and House, P. (1977) The 'false consensus effect': an egocentric bias in social perception and attribution processes, *Journal of Experimental Psychology*, 13, 279–301.

Ross, L., Lepper, M. R. and Hubbard, M. (1975) Perseverance in self-perception and social perception: biased attributions in the debriefing paradigm, *Journal of Personality and Social Psychology*, 32, 880–92.

Ross, L. and Nisbett, R. E. (1991) *The Person and the Situation: Perspectives of Social Psychology*, New York: McGraw-Hill.

Rothbart, M. (1981) Memory processes and social beliefs. In D. Hamilton (ed.), *Cognitive Processes in Stereotyping and Intergroup Behaviour*, Hillsdale, NJ: Erlbaum.

Rotter, J. B. (1966) Generalised expectancies for internal versus external control of reinforcement, *Psychological Monographs*, 80.

—— (1982) *The Development and Application of Social Learning Theory*, New York: Praeger.

Rowatt, W. C., Cunningham, M. R. and Druen, P. B. (1998) Deception to get a date, *Personality and Social Psychology Bulletin*, 24, 286–306.

Rudisill, M. E. (1988) The influences of causal dimension orientations and perceived competence on adult's expectations, persistence, performance and the selection of causal dimensions, *International Journal of Sport Psychology*, 19, 184–98.

Runciman, W. G. (1966) *Relative Deprivation and Social Justice*, London: Routledge and Kegan Paul.

Ruscher, J. B. (1998) Prejudice and stereotyping in everyday communications. In M. P. Zanna (ed.), *Advances in Experimental Social Psychology*, vol. 30, San Diego: Academic Press.

Ruscher, J. B. and Hammer, E. D. (1994) Revising disrupted impressions through conversation, *Journal of Personality and Social Psychology*, 66, 530–41.

Schank, R.C. and Abelson, R.P. (1977) *Scripts, Plans, Goals and Understanding: An Inquiry into Human Knowledge Structures*, Hillsdale, NJ: Erlbaum.

Schiffman, R. and Wicklund, R. A. (1992) The minimal group paradigm and its minimal psychology, *Theory and Psychology*, 2, 29–50.

Schlenker, B. R., Weigold, M. F. and Hallam, J. R. (1990) Self-serving attributions in social context: effects of self-esteem and social pressure, *Journal of Personality and Social Psychology*, 58, 855–63.

Schneider, D. J. (1973) Implicit personality theory: a review, *Psychological Bulletin*, 79, 294–309.

Schneider, K. and Unzer, L. (1992) Preschooler's attention and emotion in an achievement and an effect game: a longitudinal study, *Cognition and Emotion*, 6, 37–63.

Seligman, M. E. P., Abramson, L. Y., Semmel, A. and Van Baeger, C. (1979) Depressive attributional style, *Journal of Abnormal Psychology*, 88, 242–7.

Shaver, K. G. (1985) *The Attribution of Blame: Causality, responsibility and blameworthiness*, New York: Springer-Verlag.

Sherif, M. (1966) *Group Conflict and Co-operation: Their Social Psychology*, London: Routledge and Kegan Paul.

Skitka, L. J. and Tetlock, P. E. (1993) Providing public assistance: cognitive and motivational processes underlying liberal and conservative policy preferences, *Journal of Personality and Social Psychology*, 65, 1205–25.

Slavin, R. E. (1983) *Co-operative Learning*, New York: Longman.

—— (1983) When does co-operative learning increase student achievement? *Psychological Bulletin*, 94, 429–45.

Slovic, P., Fischhoff, B. and Lichtenstein, S. (1982) Facts versus fears: understanding perceived risk. In D. Kahneman, P. Slovic and A. Tversky (eds), *Judgement Under Uncertainty: Heuristics and Biases*, New York: Cambridge University Press.

Smith, E. E., Adams, N. and Schorr, D. (1978) Fact retrieval and the paradox of inference, *Cognitive Psychology*, 10, 438–64.

Smith, E. R. and Mackie, D. M. (1995) *Social Psychology*, New York: Worth.

Smith, P. B. and Harris Bond, M. (1998) *Social Psychology across cultures*, 2nd edn, London: Prentice Hall.

Smith, P., Magaro, P. and Pederson, S. (1983) Clinical types in a normal publication: concurrent and construct validity, *Journal of Clinical Psychology*, 39, 498–506.

Sperber, D. (1985) Anthropology and psychology: toward an epidemiology of representations, *Man*, 20, 73–89.

Stangor, C., Lynch, L., Dunn, C. and Glass, B. (1992) Categorisation of individuals on the basis of multiple social features, *Journal of Personality and Social Psychology*, 62, 207–18.

Storms, M. D. (1973) Videotape and the attribution process: reversing actors' and observers' points of view, *Journal of Personality and Social Psychology*, 27, 65–175.

Surim, J. K., Askin, K. J., Hall, W. S. and Hunter, B. A. (1995) Sexism and racism: old-fashioned and modern prejudices, *Journal of Personality and Social Psychology*, 68, 199–214.

Tajfel, H. (1970) Experiments in intergroup discrimination, *Scientific American*, 223, 96–102.

—— (ed.) (1978) *Differentiation between Social Groups: Studies in the Social Psychology of Intergroup Relations*, London: Academic Press.

Tajfel H. and Billig, M. (1974) Familiarity and categorisation of intergroup behaviour, *Journal of Experimental Social Psychology*, 10, 159–70.

Tajfel, H. and Turner, J. C. (1986) The social identity theory of intergroup behaviour. In S. Worchel and L. W. Austin (eds), *Psychology of Intergroup Relations*, Chicago: Nelson-Hall.

Taylor, S. E. (1995) *Health Psychology*, 3rd edn, New York: McGraw-Hill.

Taylor, S. E., Lichtman, R. R. and Wood, J. V. (1984) Attributions, beliefs about control, and adjustment to breast cancer, *Journal of Personality and Social Psychology*, 46, 499–502.

Thompson, S. C. (1981) Will it hurt if I can control it? A complex answer to a simple question, *Psychological Bulletin*, 52, 415–24.

Thornton, B. (1984) Defensive attribution of responsibility: evidence for an arousal-based motivational bias, *Journal of Personality and Social Psychology*, 46, 721–34.

Triandis, H. C., McCusker, C. and Hui, C. H. (1990) Multi-method probes of individualism and collectivism, *Journal of Personality and Social Psychology*, 59, 1006–20.

Tripathi, R. C. and Srivastava, R. (1981) Relative deprivation and intergroup attitudes, *European Journal of Social Psychology*, 11, 313–18.

Triplet, R. G. (1992) Discriminatory biases in the perception of illness: the application of availability and representativeness heuristics to the AIDS crisis, *Basic and Applied Social Psychology*, 13, 303–22.

Turner, J. C. (1982) Towards a cognitive redefinition of the social group. In H. Tajfel (ed.), *Social Identity and Intergroup Relations*, Cambridge: Cambridge University Press.

—— (1985) Social categorisation and the self concept: a social cognitive theory of group behaviour. In E. J. Lawler (ed.), *Advances in Group Processes: Theory and Research*, vol. 2, Greenwich, CT: JAI Press.

Turner, J. C., Hogg, M. A., Oakes, P. J., Reicher, S. D. and Wetherell, M. S. (1987) *Rediscovering the Social Group: A Self-Categorisation Theory*, Oxford: Blackwell.

Turnquist, D. C., Harvey, J. H. and Anderson, B. L. (1988) Attributions and adjustments to life-threatening illness, *British Journal of Clinical Psychology*, 27, 55–66.

Tversky, A. and Kahneman, D. (1974) Judgement under uncertainty: heuristics and biases, *Science*, 185, 1124–31.

Tyerman, A. and Spencer, C. (1983) A critical test of the Sherif's Robber's Cave experiment: intergroup competition and co-operation between groups of well acquainted individuals, *Small Group Behaviour*, 14, 515–31.

Vanneman, R. D. and Pettigrew, T. F. (1972) Race and relative deprivation in the urban United States, *Race*, 13, 461–86.

Walker, I. and Pettigrew, T. E. (1984) Relative deprivation theory: an overview and conceptual critique, *British Journal of Social Psychology*, 23, 301–10.

Weiner, B. (1979) A theory of motivation for some classroom experiences, *Journal of Educational Psychology*, 71, 3–25.

—— (1986) *An Attribution Theory of Motivation and Emotion*, New York: Springer-Verlag.

—— (1995) *Judgements of Responsibility*, New York: Guildford.

White, S. A. (1993) The effect of gender and age on causal attribution in softball players, *International Journal of Sport Psychology*, 24, 49–58.

Worchel, S., Andreoli, V. A. and Folger, R. (1977) Intergroup co-operation and intergroup attraction: the effect of previous interaction and outcome of combined effect, *Journal of Experimental Social Psychology*, 13, 131–40.

Worchel, S., Cooper, J. and Goethels, G. R. (1988) *Understanding Social Psychology*, 4th edn, Chicago: Darsey.

Wright, S. C., Taylor, D. M. and Moghaddam, F. M. (1990) Responding to membership in a disadvantaged group: from acceptance to collective protest, *Journal of Personality and Social Psychology*, 58, 994–1003.

Wurf, E. and Markus, H. (1983) Cognitive consequences of the negative self. Presented at the annual meeting of the American Psychological Association, Anaheim, California.

Zebrowitz, L. A. (1990) *Social Perception*, Pacific Grove, CA: Brooks/Cole.

Zucker, G. S. and Weiner, B. (1993) Conservation and perceptions of poverty: an attributional analysis, *Journal of Applied Social Psychology*, 23, 925–43.

Index